Mason Jars…

"A MOUNTAIN MEMOIR"…
…From The Hills

Joe Mason

Mason Jars…

"A MOUNTAIN MEMOIR"…
…From The Hills

Joe Mason

Second Printing

Copyright © 2011
All Rights Reserved

PUBLISHED BY:
BRENTWOOD CHRISTIAN PRESS
WWW.BRENTWOODBOOKS.COM
1-800-334-8861

INTRODUCTION

We have come to the end of the first decade of the new millennium which already is becoming old hat. Most of us are getting used to saying "twenty" … whatever number it is as the years go by, and I might add quicker than I had planned.

Though the decade seemed to move faster than most, it took time to produce some strange but astonishingly frightful happenings. We started out the "two's" with a new president … another of the Bush variety, this one younger and a bit more brash than father Bush. First time there's been a son following in father's footsteps since back in the days of the "Adams family" … (duh, duh, duh, dum - click click) … Okay, so you don't remember that Adams family.

Then barely into his job, Bush the younger had to deal with the worst tragedy of our country's life, 9/11. That scurrilous act virtually changed this decade from the get-go. Some for the better, some for the worse. But I shan't discuss the whys and wherefores of those days here. Suffice to say they were terrifying and at this point, thankfully, we're looking on to our future.

Just a few years later there was the hurricane, Katrina, and the "flood of all floods" - a natural devastation of such huge proportions that it almost obliterated New Orleans. I wondered if it would destroy the French Quarter and old Preservation Hall, that unique musical wonder of Dixieland jazz that I discovered in the mid-1960s. However, as we usually have done in this country for over 200 years, resiliency and much help from all around took over the exhilarating spirit of that city and as we now enter the 2nd decade of this century, New Orleans is breathing pretty normally again.

Then comes a thing called the worst "recession" since the great depression. Produced a lot of angst and turmoil for many - the young, the middle, and the older. I suppose, even at this writing, some of the terrible aftermath is still hanging around many corners of the country. But again, the resiliency of the American spirit is taking hold once more and gains, economically, financially, educationally, and, heaven help us, maybe even politically are beginning to move to the up side. But I shall not be "prognosticational" on these pages about areas of which I have little expertise. I leave that to the professional pundits and move on to the real purpose of this little book.

I have decided, instead, to present in this little book a *memoir,* most of which relates to this first decade. Before you lose your equilibrium from laughter, let me explain.

This past decade didn't turn out quite like I planned it. But then, I'm not sure I had any hard and fast plans on the books ahead of time for the past ten years, anyway. You see, at the very beginning ... mid-2000 A.D. to be exact, I retired. If I had a plan, it was merely to travel around the countryside and bring a little humor, laughs, impressions, and piano playing to audiences young and old. As it turned out, most of the audiences were older, but so was I, so I fit right in. That plan has worked out pretty well and I am still able to share a laugh here and there, thanks be to God.

The part of the "plan" I had not counted on happened around four years after I retired. My dear wife, Virginia, who retired sometime after I did, had expressed her desire to live in the mountains of north Georgia. She, lovely woman that she is, was born and raised in Atlanta. We met in Decatur at Evan's Fine Foods. At the time, of course, I was not aware of her mountain desires. I was only aware of her. That was good enough for me. Still is.

However, after years in the city, she decided to "lift up her eyes unto the hills from whence cometh her help," and forthwith upon retirement, started snooping around the highways and hedges, looking for a possible abode in the mountains. In the process, she found a little piece of property along with a builder with a plan, we agreed that it was the thing to do at the time and some months later, "poof," we moved into a community called Skylake, a few miles up behind the "Old Sautee Store" not far from beautiful downtown Helen. I thought it was kinda cool.

However, my above-mentioned "plan" had not included mountain hillsides, cutting firewood in the winter, blowing five trillion leaves each fall, and having no Waffle House within walking distance. Nor did it include the possibility of herds of flower-consuming deer traipsing through my yard, followed by rafters of turkeys gobbling, northern geese a-honking, or sneaky snakes a-slithering.

Additionally, I struggle with no city newspaper and will expend time and much gas to drive closer to the metropolis to fetch one. And if worse comes to worst, I will travel many miles on a "waffle run" to the closest Waffle House to imbibe in a "dark one" with crispy bacon on the side, and a cup of "joe" for Joe, even when the gas is pushing $4 a gallon.

So, in an effort to "blend in" to the landscape around, and become a part of the community around me, I have attempted to embrace mountain living. And for me, one way to be more blended with the fellow mountain folk is to write about various and sundry aspects of the mountain life I have observed and become a part of. I had written for some years for a local paper in Decatur where I worked and thought I would try again. Hence, you have before you a veritable kaleidoscope of sights and sounds of life in the mountains for me, as seen through the "Mason Jar" mentality.

To be quite honest, I suppose one could debate the "memoir" aspect of this presentation. Mr. Webster presents the definition of the word, memoir, as "a narrative composed from personal experience," and also, "an account of something noteworthy." And so, it is clearly up to you, the reader, as to whether the following pieces measure up to Mr. Webster's definition so stated. They do honestly represent some of the more exhilarating occurrences and day by day observations that I have experienced while living out the last part of the first decade of this new century up in the mountains of north Georgia.

However, it behooves me to be admittedly forthright about this treatise. Had it not been for the good graces of Mr. Billy Chism, the editor of the White County News paper, which covers the county like the dew, and his willingness to include the contents herein to be printed in said paper over the past few years, it is a good possibility, if not total probability, that I would have nothing wherewith to fill the following pages. As a result, there would be no jar, no opinions, no blending in, and no memoir to read, define, or even wonder about.

In other words, thanks to editor Chism, these essays of features, opinions, and captivating minutia of this small but, hopefully, interesting book were first published in the county paper and now are herewith included to further enhance my "memoirability." Old news, you might say. Well, yes, but an essay is an essay is an essay, and can be so placed in perpetuity. Thus, you have a collection of past columns which I trust will bring some bit of enjoyment to you and your funny bone. Not all of them are absolutely funny, some are rather funny, and some, I suppose, are not so funny. Not everyone has the same funny bone.

Some of my readers may be aware that this so-called mountain memoir is my fourth book of the "Mason Jar" series. In all probability, it will be the last. I seriously considered trying to make a deal with a big time publisher, like, Simon & Schuster or Random House, but they might scoff at the idea and think better of it. In fact, they probably would think nothing of it. So, I decided to do it myself, which meant, if I want to write a memoir, I can write a memoir. And if you want to read it, that is strictly up to you.

However, I believe you will maintain some enjoyment as you make your way through these snippets of life in the mountains. And if you ever decide to visit the territory here and about, I share a bit of wisdom that I picked up soon after I became part of the landscape … . to wit, always remember, there's nothing like a good horseback ride through the trails to make you feel better off.

TABLE OF CONTENTS

PART III -
PRAYING WHAT HAPPENS WASHINGTON STAYS IN WASHINGTON

PART IV -
FAMILY STILL THE MOST IMPORTANT

PART V -
THE BENEDICTION

PART I -

MOUNTAINOUS HAPPENINGS GALORE

THE HILLS ARE ALIVE WITH THE SOUND OF SNEEZING

As you know, the chlorophyll-laden leaves have sprouted into their spring finery over the hill and dale, sending allergy sufferers scurrying for relief in various and sundry places. Doesn't matter, you can run, but the oak and pine pollen will find you.

Recently, I even traveled way down below the gnat line for some relief, but the pollen and sneezin' followed me. I caught some cool breezes on the coast. Then I sneezed at the breeze. Didn't really do much good, just made my sneezin' worse. Must have been seaweed pollen.

For some reason, my sneeze pattern has changed. What for years was one or two short sneezes and a couple of Ahhs, just before the "Big Kahoona," has changed to the point where my Ahhhs increased some five-fold. What this means is, I suck in so many "Ahhs," that when the "Big Kahoona" finally does blow, I think my esophagus and all other throat parts will explode.

Worried about this change, I did some research on the sneeze subject. I found that a sneeze is "a semi-autonomous, convulsive expulsion of air from the lungs through the nose and mouth, most commonly caused by foreign particles irritating the nasal mucosa" - causing the slimy mucus, better known as you know what which rhymes with shot..

The foreign particles of course, would be the culprits, slyly stealing their way into certain parts of your existence, as they silently, yea, invisibly wander through the cracks and crevices, ever-vigilantly migrating within and stashing their goods deep in your passages, and then, "Boom," to quote John Madden the football announcer, they start going off. This is not a political definition regarding our immigration policy, but merely foreign nose irritants.

Furthermore, I found that the "reason for the sneezin'" which lurks about is not just the expelling activity of the nose and mouth and upper body parts, urged on by these foreign particles agitating all that is within you. But instead, may be something altogether different than one expects and relates to the response we receive from fellow sufferers, i.e. "God bless you."

Years ago, this phrase, "God bless you," or more likely, "God Help you," came from "various and sundry superstitions relating to evil spirits that crept into ones soul," and that when one sneezes, one is in effect sneezing out those evil spirits or sins, if you will, thus cleansing the body in the process.

I suppose, then, that when I sneezed yesterday while walking off the green, after I had spoken harshly to my ball for not going into the hole like I wanted, and my partner responded, "God bless you," perhaps that meant I could start the next hole with a clean slate. Well, it's a comforting thought anyway.

So, now that I live in the hills of north Georgia and because my sneezing mechanism has changed and my final "Big Kahoona" is now even bigger, I am wondering if this is caused by a long build-up of evil spirits which have gathered in my deep recesses and need more desperately to come out, like an exorcism of some kind.

Excuse me, ahh, aahh, Ahh, AAHH ... BOOM! ... . . God bless me!

A TAX ON BOVINE AROMATIC HABITS?

Back in early December 007, somewhere between the crowning of Sir Obama and the first showing of Santa Claus, there was an article in the paper about an arm of the government reaching out to financially corral the aromatic habits of cows. Yep, only in Washington.

The agency, known by its trademark initials - EPA - seems to be making an attempt to assess fees - read, cow tax - from the cow owners in an attempt to curtail the poor cow's natural habits from "both ends," so to speak, thus, ridding the environment of certain unseemly bovine-induced belching and flatulence. And there are a lot of cows up here who daily and freely express themselves.

This notion, by the way, comes with the approval of none other than a 2007 Supreme Court ruling that the cow's "green-house gases emitted by belching and flatulence amounts to air pollution." There was no mention of whether the cows in question were of the Republican variety or Democratic variety, but back in 2007, it probably didn't matter.

At this point in time, the possibility of the EPA's assessment is aimed only toward milk cows and beef cattle, as well as a few errant pigs running around the barnyard "root-hogging or dying," poor things. There was no mention of other livestock such as, horses, mules, llamas, billy-goats, nanny-goats or chickens to be included in this so-called tax assessment.

And I am happy to say that up to now, the agency in question has made no movement to assess humans for any, er, uh, unwanted or unobtrusive odorous polluting of the air, though I'm not sure I trust this arm of the government when it comes to snooping or sniffing for other creative ways to raise money. They seem ever vigil at keeping their noses in the air, sniffing out every possible way to extract more dollars from our pockets.

Back to the poor, innocent cows. I have had limited experience with the bovine category of livestock, except for being kicked in the stomach once as a wee person while my grandpappy was milking his sweet Bessie. And therefore, I have never heard any such cow belching or been close enough to a cow when he or she exercised their, uh, flatulent prerogative. I figure that the cow has a right to freely succumb to mother nature's power over their bovine digestive system when and wherever they so choose.

But I feel for our dear farmers, who could be out hundreds, even thousands of dollars in fees - i.e., subtle cow tax amounts - due to, let's see, how can I put this, er, their cow's air polluting aromatic waste. They're talking over $100 per cow, for goodness sakes. Just for cow digestive habits. That's a lot money for a "bad air day."

And how are they going to know which cow just goes ahead and unconsciously "lets it fly," thus polluting the air around and which cow has a more acceptable hygiene manner, discreetly expressing mother nature's handiwork. And how much should each cow be allowed such expression, anyway? Perhaps they will employ a flatulence meter reader, checking herds. Not sure I'd want that job, regardless of the high unemployment rating.

So, write your congressman, call your representative, and take up signs and placards and support the animal rights of the bovine population. It's got to stop somewhere. Like I've said, next thing you know government noses will come snooping and sniffing around our homes. And that should be my own personal "no smell zone."

BEAUTIFUL HORSES STIR CHILDHOOD MEMORIES

If I had it to do over again, one thing I would do is learn to ride a horse. Of course, the first thing I would have to do would be run away from home. My father rode horseback as a young man. But my mother rode the piano bench. As a result, I learned to ride the bench, too.

I did have a medium-size pony once that we kept on my grandfather's farm. Her name was Trixie. She stood somewhere between Trigger and the pony that Rhett Butler gave Bonnie Blue, big enough that I had to climb up on the stump out by the hen house to get in the saddle.

One day we were trying to get the bridle on her and she kicked me. Not bad, but it hurt enough that I probably cried, as most 8-year-olds would. Mother was watching. From then on it was the piano bench for me. I guess she was afraid I might get kicked in the head and not know middle C from the key of G. That's not good when you're riding the piano bench.

Anyway, I bring all this up because of all the beautiful horses up here in the county in which we now live. They remind me of my home state of Kentucky. Recently, Sir William Chism, our great editor, alluded to the wisteria on an old barn out on highway 255. One day while riding by and noticing the barn in question, I also noticed four very beautiful and friendly horses, grazing nearby.

I say friendly because I decided to stop by the pasture and walked up to the fence for a closer look-see. One of the horses was near and walked toward me and the next thing I knew, here came the other three in a trot. They came close enough for me to pet them on the nose and use some Lone Ranger talk, like, "Whoa, big fellow." Because I didn't have anything to feed them, I presume they became disinterested in my company and soon turned and continued their daily habit of grazing.

It was a small victory in my quandary of life with a horse. For some reason, horses I have been around have not been all that friendly. It started with Trixie, my one and only pony-horse. Later, as a young adult, I tried to pet a horse on the nose one time and it about bit my hand off.

Another time I was attending a meeting out in New Mexico. Several of us decided to go horseback riding at this trail place, similar to what you might notice up in the Nachooche valley. We were city dudes acting out. The horse I rode kept turning his head back and biting my tennis shoe on the toe sticking out of the stirrup. He probably thought I had no business riding a horse with tennis shoes. Anyway, it wasn't all that happy of an experience.

I admire people who can ride. I have two lady friends who live down the street. They each have a horse. They ride tall in the saddle. One day I saw one of my friends riding bare-back. She can even ride tall without a saddle, I thought. I was envious.

The other day I read about a young girl in Gainesville who has been an equestrian since she was a kid. When she was about 13, the horse she was riding threw her and dragged her around for a time while she dangled with one foot caught in the stirrup. She overcame the experience as well as a concussion and now has a scholarship to University of Georgia's Equestrian team.

What riding courage, I thought. If that had happened to me, I doubt that my mother would have even let me ride the piano bench. Might fall off and hurt myself.

When it comes to horses, I'm just a poor romantic, living out the lines of Willie Nelson's song ... "I grew up a-dreaming - of being a cowboy - and loving the cowboy ways..." But I suppose fate dealt me another Nelson tune, to wit ... "Mamas, don't let your babies grow up to be cowboys."

A GOOD DEED CAN DIVERT YOUR ATTENTION

While munching on a plentiful breakfast at Waffle House some miles away, my wife and I glanced to see a very elderly couple enter and sit close by. He sat quietly while she read the menu choices, then gave the order to the waitress, and then lead in a brief blessing when the food came.

We soon left and stopped for gas at a service station close by. While leaning against my truck as the gas was pumping in the tank, the same elderly couple from the restaurant drove up on the other side of the pumps. The gentleman got out from the passenger side, picked up the nozzle and stood, looking at the numbers and choices on the side of the pump. He seemed perplexed. His elderly wife had exited the driver's side and came around to look-see, also.

My boy scout training kicked in. Remembering the line in my oath of years ago that says, "To help other people at all times," I stepped over and asked, "May I help?"

"I can't get the numbers off," he said, referring to the previous sale amount on the pump.

"Are you going to use a credit card?" I asked

He produced it and said, "Yes."

I told him where to slide in the card which he did and then how to flip up the lever for the type gas he wanted. He seemed completely confused but soon saw that the "numbers" went away and zeros appeared on the little screen indicating it was time for him to pump his gas.

"Now, place it in the tank and pull the lever," I explained.

He followed my instructions and I helped him push down the little tab to keep the nozzle running until it was filled. He smiled, but never said a word.

At that point, his wife began to talk about not being able to "understand these new-fangled gadgets." It seemed as if they had never seen a place to pump gas before, but I think they just wanted to make this "old" boy scout feel good about his good deed.

I waited until he was finished and showed him where to get his receipt, bid them adieu, turned and went back over to my vehicle. I got in the seat and was about to shut the door when my wife, who had been watching this whole scene and, being ever-mindful of my brain cell deficiency, said, "Did you finish pumping your gas?"

"Oops," I thought. In the meantime, my gas had finished pumping and the nozzle was still hanging in the tank, waiting for the absent-minded person of said vehicle to replace it and take his own receipt. If my sweet wife had not reminded me of my own gas-pumping, I would probably have blissfully driven off with the hose stuck in my tank, and like little Jack Horner, contemplating what a good-old boy scout I was.

Boy Scout training is a very wholesome way to help young people grow up to be responsible, useful citizens. Even though I didn't go very far up the "scout ladder," I'm glad I learned to be helpful to others.

I'm also glad I married such a lovely and sweet wife who helps me remember who I am and why I'm here. One day, she will be able to read the menu to me, order my breakfast, and say the blessing before we eat. I'll have to worry later about how we're going to pump whatever gas we have left to pump.

EXTRA SET OF KEYS
CAN SAVE ON GAS

A few days ago, before the new "super-duper" Wal Mart opened, I made a trip over to the old Wal Mart on 441 to pick up a couple of items. It is still open and alive with the sound of "specials in the hosiery section on aisle 13." But who knows for how long. It may soon become a building for a week-end flea market.

I pulled into the parking lot behind a rather tattered pick-up with a camper on top. I could see a variety of things cluttered in the back of the camper, as if it had seen lots of rough-road traveling, while shopping or camping or sightseeing around the country. The bumper stickers gave some indication regarding the owner's take on life, liberty and the pursuit of free health care.

One sticker said "Back off, man, I'm a scientist!" Another read, "Earth first - we'll screw up the other planets later." Still another said "Have you hugged your goat today?" There were a couple more, but this is a family news paper and the editorial people have their limits.

As I stepped out of my truck, I realized the motor was running in the vehicle in question. My first thought, of course, was that some poor soul had inadvertently left his or her keys in the ignition, hastily hopped out, probably in a hurry to get to the hosiery section, and dashed off, oblivious to the motor still running. If I had thought about it long and hard enough I might have remembered doing the same thing, but I'm didn't want to think about it that long.

Thinking about my Boy Scout training days once again, I decided to do my good deed for the day, step up and check to see if the door was locked and if not, reach in and turn off the motor and take the keys in and ask the "announcing lady" to share over the loud speaker that someone's keys are at the desk, giving the license number, etc. But just then, the owner rolled his basket up before I could do my deed.

"I just noticed that your motor was running," I uttered, as cheerfully as possible, "and was about to see if the car was locked in an effort to help," hoping he wouldn't think me too forward.

"I have another key." he said. "If I turn the motor off, I have a difficult time starting it again. So, I just let it run and keep an extra set of keys in my pocket to unlock it."

He quickly loaded his things, evidently not interested in small talk, hopped in, and was off like a "herd of goats," which I suppose he would hug if he felt the urge, according to his bumper sticker. I also gathered from his long, white outer coat that he may have been just exactly what another bumper sticker indicated - a scientist - and really wanted me to "back off" so he could load up and leave.

I think there is a lesson or two here. First, it's best not to wear a long white coat out in public. Someone may think you're a scientist and want to start a long harangue about whether you're a "creation scientist" or an "evolution scientist," and either way, your nice white coat may get a bit mussed up. Then again, they might think you're a doctor and health care is not something to discuss in the parking lot on a hot day.

A second lesson is to always carry an extra set of car keys in your pocket or purse. If you can't start your car, go get it fixed and that will take care of that. But you also might be absent-minded, like myself, and in a hurry to get to the special at the hosiery section and leave your motor running, which may cause people to ask, "Did you hug your goat today?"

BEWARE THE TURKEY
ON THE PROWL

If the good White County News hits the streets on time, then you would know that yesterday was Halloween. Boohoo! You also may know that the day after is "All Saints Day," so-called for the saints who have no special day named in their honor. Which means that some of you don't get any holidays, I guess.

What you may not know, however, is that two days after Halloween is known as "The Day of the Dead." And this brings me to my subject for consideration … the lowly, not-so-good-looking, shuffling along, bird-for-the-season and pride of every Thanksgiving dinner table - the turkey! Ready, aim…

Already, I may be in the cross hairs of PETA, the national support group for animals, for making disparaging remarks about this annually designated "fowl of the month" for November. I mean no harm to the old bird. It's merely a November warning for consumers who have the tendency to consume, as it were, parts of the plucked butterball at various and sundry times during the month of November, yea even December as well.

A warning, you say? Yes, and it comes from far off yonder in the northeastern territory of Brookline, Massachusetts, located in the inner recesses of Boston. I heard an interview on the radio with the district chief of police of that fair community about the struggle his minions are having in their neighborhoods with "wild" turkeys on the loose.

I don't suppose you could say a turkey strolling down the sidewalk in town is considered wild, buy when he - or she, as the case may be - decides to "attack" some indiscriminate pedestrian, then, I would think said turkey could fall into the category of the "day of the dead," and quickly go from wild turkey (not to be confused with the bourbon of the same name) to Thanksgiving butterball.

Not so, says the chief of Brookline. No "day of the dead" turkeys there. In the interview I heard, he suggested that one should move away from said wild turkey, run, if one can outrun an attacking turkey, or, get this, hit him (or her) with a purse! I'm not making this up, folks. According to the story, turkeys were in fact roaming through the community and some must have been angry enough (read, "I'm gonna peck your eyes out before you shoot me for your dinner") to attack some poor innocent passersby who probably had nothing on their minds remotely considering this to be a "day of the dead" for the turkey.

I have never encountered an angry turkey. My only experience of any bird angry at me was as a wee lad, some four or five years of age, being chased by the mean, white leghorn rooster on my Grandpa's farm. We finally ate that sucker for Sunday lunch. I gleefully had the "pulley bone." And if you do not know what a pulley bone is, I feel sorry for you.

Back to the turkey. There are many turkeys in the area where I live. They stroll through our yard by the half-dozen or more. They do not appear to be angry or in any way raise their ugly head, and I do mean ugly, and move toward me or anyone else in an attack mode. Actually, they are going to my neighbor's backyard for some corn that they throw out for them. What's to be angry about?

I'm glad we live in a safe community, free from the worry of combative turkeys ready to pick a fight. I would hate to have to call the chief of police in our fair city and ask him for help because I'm being attacked by an angry turkey who may think I have a "day of the dead" vendetta toward him, only to hear the chief tell me that I could run away and into the house or hit the turkey with my purse.

DON'T FORGET TO PAT DOWN YOUR TURKEY

There's a lot of angst over being patted down at the airport these days. Lots of people are traveling around the country and invariably one must take to the skies now and then. Some people fly weekly. And in addition, the Thanksgiving traveling season is right around the corner and the newly inaugurated security rules are being viewed rather warily by passengers.

Of course, in an effort to make the country safe, the TSA boys are going through the rituals of security checks at every airport. Lately, they not only make you go through the metal detector - as it was called in the old days - and take your shoes, belts, and coats off, but your ear-rings, watches, and gold teeth out. Now, however, if they think you might be "up to something," they pat you down in places you haven't been patted since your mama powdered your bare bottom.

I suppose this is okay in order for everyone to feel safe on whatever flying machine one may have to use. But there are some among the flying public that are balking at being singled out and told to "spread 'em" while the stranger with the badge does his or her own rendition of personal "wanning" one's private territory.

But I'm not here to discuss the pros and cons of undercover underwear searchings. My question goes to the, uh, meat of the issue. We were talking about this issue in a previous essay. It comes up in the midst of most every mid-November season, and the question that remains is do you stay with that great American tradition and get your turkey ready to go under the knife? More particularly, have you learned the fine art of patting that gobbler down with the proper basting mixture, as well as flavoring those little innard parts you put in the gravy.

Just recently, I was watching Paula Dean Y'all, which you probably know to be her full name. She is the last word, it seems, at the art of culinary expediency. I would think that Ms. Y'all is such an artist at basting most anything, that she could make any turkey grin just pondering the possibility of being patted down by those dainty, southern, flour-friendly fingers of hers.

I must admit to entertaining the fantasy of patting down my own Thanksgiving turkey with whatever mixture of "parsley, sage, rosemary, and thyme" to use the song lyric, but it has yet to come to pass. The closest I ever came was one thanksgiving years ago when my dear wife was so sick with the influenza she could not budge from the bed. Most of the preparations she had done a couple of days earlier. But I had to *cook* them.

As she passed down her urgings from the bedroom covers, I gamely turned the oven on to the proper setting, stirred the green beans profusely, and placed the pan of dressing in the oven at the right time with careful dexterity. Ms. Y'all would be proud of me.

The best part, however, was that I did not have to pat down the turkey, lucky fowl. My sister-in-law had that chore as she had done for some years. No one messed with the turkey but my sis-in-law. She would rival dear Paula, with her own touch of southern drawl. All I remember doing was taking what I had "cooked" to her house and eating there, leaving the poor patient in our bed at home with nothing more than her misery. Not even a pat-down.

TALES OF OUTDOOR ADVENTURES

Ever wonder how someone could kill a bear like Jeremiah Johnson did or bring down a caribou with a lever-action Winchester '73 or hit three ducks in a row with a Remington automatic 16-gauge? You could call these big time adventurous exploits.

At a social gathering recently, a few of us guys gathered over in a corner and started telling some tales of adventure. One told of hunting quail in south Georgia and bagging the limit with family members and friends. My experience at bird hunting was well-documented on my uncle's farm years ago with my grand single-barrel shotgun. Missed my one chance - at one bird.

Another told of his outdoor expedition in Montana, hunting elk and moose and maybe a wooly mammoth … not with a 30-30 magnum Howitzer which most hunters use to bring down such big game, but with a bow and arrow … call it bow-hunting. Shucks, I couldn't even hit the garage where my target was nailed when I was a kid.

Then somebody told about trolling around the edge of a big lake, and hooking a large 20-inch catfish, using something like a hi-ho silver spinner worm-a-doodle of some kind.

Even though I've moved to the mountains of north Georgia, it doesn't mean I have now become a true, "daddy-grizzly" in the woods, ready to take on any and all big game to bring home and hang in the living room over the mantle. I mean, having dominion over the fish, fowl, and "every living creature that moves on the ground," as the Good Book says, doesn't mean I'm all that proficient or even interested in messing with, say a bull moose charging in my direction.

My adventurous spirit seems more in line with a friend whom I saw fishing the other day as I passed a small lake close to home. Out of character, I thought. Usually, I see him murderously cutting a tennis ball out of the reach of his opponent. I glanced a little further down the slope of the lake, and lo, there was his wife, casting in another direction.

I didn't know they fished, let alone together. My wife and I went fishing one time but we weren't very good at it. That is to say, we brought home an empty bucket. Went out for pizza later. I'm better at swinging a golf club than casting about in the water for some crafty fish. Yes, I know, some would debate the point.

Back to my angler friends and "the rest of the story." I was told later that my friend noticed a small boat at water's edge, pushed it into the water and then attempted to step in, I suppose to get a closer look at the fish. The boat was not moored as well as it should have been and slowly drifted "out to sea" as he stepped in. He found himself like Charlie Chaplin of old, with one foot in the boat and one foot still on land, discovering at the most inopportune time that he was half-way in and halfway out ... . . and to make matters worse, without a paddle.

Now, most people who fish in a boat and experience some mishap, as I understand it, may fall *out* of a boat. In this case, my friend fell *in* it. Basically his mishap set the boat adrift, and he, with no paddle, started drifting away from shore. He quickly called up his past Marine training - as well as hollering for his wife - grabbed a stick floating by and began to "stick" his way back to land. But alas, the stick broke.

The story ends with his dear wife coming to the rescue and bringing him back to safety. I didn't have the heart to ask how she did that, but knowing her fishing prowess, I could imagine she cast out toward his skiff, hooked it securely, and reeled him in to land where he stepped out, alive and able to tell about his mishap. But I doubt that he has.

I saw her a few days later and asked where he was. She said he was on a week-end fishing trip. I didn't have the heart to ask if he took a paddle. Don't want to spoil an outdoor adventure.

RUMORS ARE FLYING
ABOUT THE HILLSIDE

The question today is to guess what is being planned for the side of the hill, just passed the Indian Mound right across the road from the cows. It has been the topic of much conversation and the cows all seem to be looking in that direction, like somebody's up to somethin'.

I realize that most people are not the least interested what will be on that hillside, nor whether the cows are looking north, south, east, or west. But it has produced as much conversation as the new Wal Mart did when it went up on 'tother side of Cleveland.

The first time I noticed workers around the hill in question was when the little man in the middle of the road twirled the slow/stop at me. While stopped, I looked up on the side of the hill at this behemoth-looking earth mover while it moved earth, trees, rocks, brush, and virtually anything else it could grab and haul off to the great land-fill in the sky, I know not where.

"What are they doing?" I asked myself. I had no answer. The little man twirling the sign didn't know. The Sautee postperson didn't know. My wife didn't know and I thought she knew everything.

A few days later, the grader-behemoth monstrosity was filling up the ditch on the other side of the road, next to the fence. Still later, that area was smoothed over and covered with straw. A few days later, the big hill had been cleared and leveled off in tiers. Trouble is, getting to the first level, would be like driving up to Brasstown Ball. Not in my pickup, thank you.

So, last week, I was riding back from dinner with some friends and when we passed the hill in question, I asked my friend, Garry B. Sokoolavich, a great real estate tycoon in White County, "What do you think they're putting up on that hill?"

"I think I heard that it's parking for the Hardiman plantation visitors," answered Mr. Sokoolavich.

"But that is such a steep incline," I said. "I'll bet people with walkers would have a tough time getting back to their car that high up. Maybe they should install a chair-lift."

"Maybe it's a heliport landing pad for that helicopter they keep complaining about in Helen," came a voice from the back seat. "The hills are alive with the sound of whirlibirds."

(Chuckles erupted).

Someone else volunteered a rumor. "I heard it might be one of those 'zip-lines" down through the cows to the Indian Mound." (Raucous laughter followed.) "Just gotta be sure no one gets dropped in a cow pie." (More laughter) "Who owns that land, anyway?"

"I believe it's owned by that developer, Marvin U. Swauve. He's working on several projects in the area, so I'm told," realtor Sokoolavich answered, "like homes and all. Maybe even a big hotel."

"Ah, a room with a view," someone chattered.

"You don't think they'd put a chicken farm up there, do you?" I asked, worriedly. "You know, they'll put those things anywhere. I can't imagine a semi-truck making it up that hill for a load of chickens, anyway."

"Nah, that won't happen," said my realtor friend. "It's probably parking for the Hardiman place. But rumors are flying here and there."

The chatter subsided and a few days later I asked someone in the know. "Well, the word I get is it'll be a pretty up-scale entrance with a turn lane, with some parking, a few homes, and possibly a big hotel. But hey, the good thing is there are no more trees there to fall across the road because of storms," he answered, with a wry smile.

Ah, friends, we can run to the hills, and hide in the woods, but the great developers in the sky will find you and dig up petunias and "put up a parking lot," as the old 60s song went. Be ever vigil. Watch the cows. And smile at the person with the stop sign. You may be crossing the "zip line."

ORANGE AND WHITE BARREL BRIGADE VANISHES

Never does one live in one place very long until the infamous orange and white barrels appear, lined up precariously in some kind of arrangement. They are there, of course, to direct your driving to and fro, while street or highway work is being processed. Such has been the case in our territory the past few months.

But while driving into town recently, I noticed they had vanished. Well, there still remains a remnant, gracing the sidewalk here and there, hiding behind an lonely mailbox, or crunched and bent from bumper damage, languishing away in a ditch close by.

I was making my way into town, ever mindful of whatever newly created "route" through the barrel brigade I might encounter, and lo and behold, they were gone ... vanished into thin air. Nary a one did I see in the roadway! And in their place was a nice smooth three-laner, appropriately lined, both yellow and white, with arrows pointing in various directions. No orange and white barrels to dodge.

And so, the newly renovated highway heading up to Helen is finished. It seemed like it started at the beginning of the new millennium. The only other evidence of "things past" that I could see was a state patrol car, patiently waiting in his obligatory perpendicular position, ready to pounce, or should I say enlighten drivers that one thing has not changed ... 35 mph. I waved in a congenial manner as I passed, pushing 36 or 37, just to get his attention.

Actually, I found the occasion a bit sad. Many was the time when I would meander through the passage of the orange and white arrangement-of-the-day barrel settings, singing, "Two hundred and ninety-nine barrels on the road ... two hundred and ninety-nine barrels ... when will they ever decide to make it ... two hundred ninety-eight barrels on the road?" I even counted the suckers once to be sure how many there were. I stopped at 299, because it fit the old "same song, second verse." I wanted to be credible with my creative barrel melody.

It wasn't easy, driving among the orange and white labyrinth, counting barrels at the same time, while singing in tempo. But I personally have become quite confident and adept at barrel driving. Living in Atlanta for many years was good training and I have driven among the best and brightest of barrels, as well as some which might be too ugly to mention. The boulevards, the side streets, the one ways and the four ways, as well as the infamous I 285, the litmus test of barrel meandering, counting, and coarse, uncouth pontificating, and I'm here to tell you that "Joe knows barrels!"

Even though they have vanished off the roadway of old 129 from ye old Huddle House to the famous Yonah Burger, they will continue to be an orange and white force to be reckoned with, dotting the road to Hel .. . er, Helen and along the mountainous curves beyond, standing all in rows, causing drivers to veer left, right, or down the middle. They may lie dormantly, discarded along the culverts and sidewalks, but make no mistake, they will rise again, usually at the whim of the ever-present road grader and flag waver, standing with his trusty "stop and slow" stick. In other words, what one road sows another road reaps. Be watchful. Stay loose. And learn to sing the barrel song. It will get you through.

One other matter I thought I'd throw in. They also did an excellent job laying sidewalks on either side of the new highway, all the way out to Yonah Burger, no less. It is a pretty far distance from downtown to walk for a hamburger, but it gives you a nice, safe walkway while you whet your appetite. I'm sure there are those who would find it a waste of money to build more sidewalks, what with the way we drive rather than walk these days. But it does remind me of a story to share which seems appropriate.

A man had just finished laying a new sidewalk A kid close by ran right through it, messing up with his small footprints. The man grabbed the boy quickly and gave him a harsh, verbal thrashing about it. A woman close by heard him and told him how awful he was to scold the little boy, asking, "Don't you like children?"

To which he retorted, "Ma'am, I like children in the abstract, but not in the concrete."

We do have a very nice roadway now on the way to Helen, be it abstract or concrete.

PARADE BRINGS BACK SCOUT EXPERIENCE

We went to the parade and festivities in town last week. Looked like most of White County did also. Never saw the like of people in one little town. Not that Cleveland is a such a little town. I was raised in a little town, and as singer Paul Simon used to warble, "In my little town…" there wasn't a lot of difference. We had similar amenities and experiences

As I was watching, I couldn't help but think of my days on the basketball team at my town's small college, dancing with the homecoming queen who rode on the back of the convertible, and remembering how difficult it was to march in the band with the base drum strapped on my shoulders, trying to beat precise march time and not trip and fall.

However, the group that called up the most vivid memory for me was the "pile" of cub scouts and boy scouts, trudging along with their leaders, and den mothers. We had a much smaller group of boy scouts in my troop and I don't think we ever walked in a parade with a fire engine, much less were seen with a group of cub scouts. They were the little kids.

We met once a week in the basement fellowship hall of the Christian Church. Our one and only leader was Mr. Gardner, the algebra teacher at the high school. He was a bachelor back at a time when being a bachelor did not produce a great deal of conversation.

Most of our meetings were spent playing "steal the bacon," a miniature version of "capture the flag," only indoors You just had to be quick enough not to get tackled on the concrete floor. Afterward, Mr. Gardner would present a merit badge to some deserving kid, lead us in reciting the scout motto, say a prayer and send us home. Sidney Prather and I would walk home in the dark and smoke at least one Old Gold cigarette he had stolen from his father. But like Bill Clinton, we had the good sense not to inhale.

One of my most vivid memories of scouting was the one and only scout camp I attended the summer I turned twelve. I say only scout camp because after that week, I gave up scouting. In order to gain the First Class ranking, scouts had to swim about fifty yards. I wasn't much of a swimmer and seemed to sink easily, which meant drowning, if I got in the deep water, out beyond the rope.

The camp was located on the premises of an armed forces airborne base close to home and our "helpers" were army personnel who were assigned that week to assist us, which meant seeing that we got out of the bunk at reveille, plopping some kind of army goulash on our tray at meal-time, and being on duty as life guards at the small lake were we swam each day.

One day, I had to perform the swim test for First Class ranking and when my turn came, I shakily jumped in and started flailing away. Things began to get blurry, (see sink easily above), and next thing I knew, there was this big hand on my bottom, pushing me up above the water line where I could breath and continue living. The sergeant whom I have always believed saved my life, muttered something about kicking harder, but it didn't register with me.

So, I soon realized that my days with Mr. Gardner and his "steal the bacon" game were over, that becoming the rank of First Class was a mere figment of my imagination because swimming was my nemesis.

The only good thing about giving up scouting was I never smoked Old Golds again. And I began developing more of an interest in basketball and the homecoming queen. Not necessarily in that order.

LOOK TWICE: MOTORCYCLES ARE EVERYWHERE!

Perhaps you have noticed lately that the mountainous roads up here are filling up with motorcycles. It seems to happen every spring, though as you know, it's fast becoming more of a year-round road activity. And they all seem to be heading for Helen. Must be the friendly "hood" for motorcycle riders.

What this means for us car/pick-up drivers is to keep a sharp eye out for the riders and riderettes. Don't want to be the cause of sending a Harley scurrying toward a ditch in search of a soft landing.

Besides, you never know who's riding a motorcycle these days. Used to, riders came out of lower California in packs, most of whom were mean looking dudes clad in Levis and leather, "varooming" down the highway, daring you to get in their way. A song from those days went something like ... "He wore black denim trousers, motorcycles boots, a black leather jacket with an eagle on the back; he had a hopped-up cycle that took off like a gun, that fool was the terror of Highway 101." Real California lore, folks. Think Marlon Brando in *The Wild One* back in the fifties.

Nowadays, your friendly motorcycle rider may be a doctor, lawyer, real estate agent, or the wife of any of the above. I even know a Georgia state legislator who rides one, but I guess I ought not to bring him up right now. I think he's retired from duty.

Believe it or not, a few years back, I, too, "had a bike" - a cool phrase from motorcycle lingo. Actually, I bought it when I turned a certain milestone age, which is none of your business. I had never owned one before. I had to wait until my parents had gone to heaven, else, my mother would have disowned me and "x-ed" me out of the family will, which included her Singer sewing machine. I never was good at sewing buttons on, anyway

When I was in high school, I saw the above-mentioned movie with Marlon Brando. I dreamed of motorcycles and leather jackets. I wanted to be cool, like Big Earl Craft, the only person in my high school who "rode" a real motorcycle to school. Nobody messed with Big Earl. He owned a thing called a service cycle. It had lots of shiny chrome and a big wide seat for Big Earl, for obvious reasons. But alas, it was not meant to be. I would never be the "terror of 23rd street" where I grew up. My parents held sway. I was sentenced to normalcy.

So, I "came of motorcycle age" late in life and rode around the north Georgia highways for a few years. Biggest problem was my knees would stick up so high, I looked like a praying mantis on wheels. Not a good image. Big Earl would have laughed.

Most bikers have that somewhat gruff look, sitting low-slung in their seats, so they look cool. Some stick their legs forward to stretch out, giving off an air of confidence. I tried that once and liked to never got my legs back in the praying mantis position. Scary.

But at least I now know what it's like to enjoy the free spirit of wheeling down the two-lane road, wind blowing in my face, bugs splatting on my sunglasses, and all the while, praying mightily, "Lord, please don't let that pick-up ahead pull out in front of me and send me catapulting over fence into that cow pasture." Not a good place to land. The Lord was gracious.

A few years back, I decided to put away childish things, after I began to see through the windshield, darkly. I also wanted to smell more mountain laurel, play more tennis, and wake up in one piece on Monday in the mountains. So, I sold the bike and quit dreaming about being the "Terror of Highway 441." But occasionally, I look longingly at a black Harley, and think of Marlon Brando, and wonder, pensively, what might have been. Yeah, I might have been in the cow pile.

When I began riding, I read of a lady who lost her son in a biker's accident. She came up with a timely bumper sticker in his memory. It said, "Look Twice, Save a Life, Motorcycles Are Everywhere."

It was a good safety precaution and she got her point across, too. I put one on my pick-up.

I thought about sticking one on my helmet while I was riding, but that's not good for your image. And Marlon would be spinning in his grave.

CHRISTMAS GIFTS ONLY
A CATALOG AWAY

Shopping for gifts during this time of year can cause one to consider becoming a modern-day Jeremiah Johnson, buying a steerage passage on a barge going north *up* the Mississippi River through Minnesota to, say, Nipawin, Saskatchewan, and never, never coming back.

Of course, that would never work for me because by the time I reached Keokuk, Iowa, I would be a frozen, skinny icicle. The cold north is not for me. I much prefer sailing around the Bahamas like Jack, my next door neighbor, did. But alas, I have no boat and there is lots of talk about hurricanes, sea monsters, and that "devil's triangle" down there. Besides, you have to go through "gator country"- with a capital G - just to get to warm water.

So, I'm destined to work out the shopping perplexity in this northern most part of this southern state as creatively as possible. Last week, I planned a trip to the malls on my way back through the city of Atlanta after a brief trip to middle Georgia. I have a few people to buy for but after tromping around two malls for almost half a day, I came away with only two small items. Not much shopping for me.

It seemed my well-made plans to do my Christmas Shopping on the way back through the big city was almost a total loss. What would I do? A trip back to the mall later? At these gas prices? Give the family members a check for a present? That's what all old folks do, usually in one of those holiday money envelops you get at the bank. That's the easy way out.

Some people do that Friday-after-Thanksgiving shopping thing at the crack of dawn. They come home with a cart full of presents. It's like last week's Dagwood comic strip. Here she comes in the door with so many presents stacked up, they covered her face. When she put them down, she realized Dagwood wasn't her husband and she was in the wrong house.

The shopping "juices" just weren't flowing for me. It got so bad at one point during my wandering at the Bass Pro Shop that I started looking at something for myself. That, of course, was not the reason I was there and all of a sudden, the "bah-humbug" spirit over-took me, momentarily. You know, when in doubt, buy something for yourself. Not a very good spirit of Christmas. Share your tree with Snoopy, Charlie Brown, it's better to give than receive, and all that.

Anyway, I came home and stood, empty-handed in the kitchen, with a mall-eyed glaze on my countenance, and then, it came to me. It was staring me full in the face, right there on the kitchen table. Stacked higher than a breadbox, cascading off the table onto a couple of chairs, and crammed down into the magazine basket ... the *catalogs!!* I had my answer. I would *order* my presents from the catalogs! What an ingenious idea.

How many times had I bad-mouthed this company and that, for sending me endless numbers of catalogs, only to run out on the porch and shout, "Thank you, Land's End, hello good old L. L. Bean, hooray Macy's, bless you Penny's and Edwin Watts, yah-hoo for the leaflets and brochures full of computers, cell phones, blackberries, raspberries, and fruit baskets to order and send for Christmas."

I felt like Jimmy Stewart, running through Bedford Falls, hollering at the buildings. I got my life back. Way to go, Clarence. I can *order* presents from the thousands of catalogs that have been sent to me all year long. It is a "wonderful life" after all. Your Christmas shopping is just a mailbox away.

Be sure you have your credit card handy, though. It's not nice to fool mother's "catalog nature."

TOUR DE GEORGIA: FRENCH FOR TOUGH PEDDLIN'?

There's a possibility that I may get some hate mail on this. I hope not, because I think my heart is in the right place. This is merely a by-stander's - and I do mean by-*stander* - observation.

It seems to me that the recently concluded "Tour de Georgia" could be an oxymoron. I am aware, of course, of the international implications for such a cycling sports event being given the name-flare, "Tour de" prefix with our state, but methinks it just doesn't fit us.

Naturally, Tour de France or Tour de Italy or Tour de Swiss Alps conjures up more of a European flavor for those fans and professionals involved in cycling. However, this is not the "South of France" where they bask in the sun on the Riviera, drinking Chateau Margeaux.

Au contraire, mon ami, this is the bedrock of the old south, a place some people feel was (maybe still is) the center of the confederacy, where chicken is king, y'all has a twang, bulldogs go "wuff, wuff," and Bubba don't ride no bicycle. Around here, peddling a herd of bicycles up to Chickamauga, Lookout Mountain, and Brasstown Bald makes you wonder if the Yankees are closing in with the cavalry.

It was, of course, a great event for Georgia, acknowledging the significance of the sport, as well as the leisure/fitness aspect of cycling. Many folks are involved in this sport. I know a nice man, rather short of stature, who rides regularly in my community. His legs reach the ground, like mine, but when he boards his bike, and climbs on that little seat-ette, they seem to dangle in the breeze. Don't see how he reaches the peddles, to say nothing of getting down.

But like Bubba, I don't ride "no bicycle, neither." I did once upon a time in another place, in another time. It began about age 10. My father, frugal-thinking man that he was, purchased me a *used* bicycle for my birthday. I had dreamed of owning a Schwinn, the Cadillac of two-wheelers, but no luck. Mine had a rather utilitarian look and was a "one-speeder," which would make peddling up to Brasstown Bald or even up to the White County court house, for that matter, totally out of the question.

I began riding it to school in the 7th grade. I thought I was cool until Harold Winders, the oldest man in our grade school, who must have been about 30, decided he wanted to use my bike to go home for lunch each day. He had the most menacing smile I ever saw … . showing about a fourth-inch of teeth and an inch and a-half of gums. One didn't argue with old Harold, and I do mean old.

Later, I rode it for my paper route, but after toppling over several times with a basket-load of papers, I decided to give it up and walk the route. When I started to high school, I gave up bike riding for good. Not cool enough. I began riding in a post-war jeep, owned by my buddy, Bill the "Crocodile," whose father was not so frugal. My peddling days were finally over.

I never owned another bicycle other than the ones purchased for my kids. Then several years ago, I gave a "three-speeder" to my wife for exercise purposes. I cannot ever remember seeing her ride it, though she may have, maybe when I was taking a nap. I tried riding it once, but the 3-inch wide seat did not fit my bony behind, and it soon became a garage sale item.   Today, I may be out of fashion, having no interest in cycling. But, I appreciate the ability and dexterity of those I see riding over hill and dale, and I make every effort to watchfully drive safely around them. At this "stage," to use the Tour de Language, I'm just a pick-up man, not a peddling man.

The good thing is I don't have to wear one of those silly looking helmet things strapped under my chin. They look like a pointed hubcap with air holes.

DAYLIGHT SAVINGS TIME TOO DARK FOR ME

Well, they've gone and messed with the time again. Now it's dark much later than usual. I liked waking up when it was light. Now, its dark again. I hate waking up in the dark. And the mountains make it seem darker. Sun comes over the mountain around 10:00. Can't see my cereal bowl, much less what's in it.

I've hated it ever since I had to wake up at 4:30 in the morning and get the papers for my delivery. My bicycle buddy, Mose Woosley, whom I've lost contact with - on purpose - talked me into taking a morning route.

You have already heard me chatter about bicycles, but I peddled around in the dark, trying to find the homes to deliver their morning paper. It was a futile effort. After two weeks, I'd had enough. I got an afternoon paper route, in the light, so I could find the houses. I haven't seen a 4:30a.m. since, except for eight week of basic training at Fort Knox, which is like a bad dream.

Now, they've changed the time and I'm waking up in the dark again. I'm not sure I understand why they mess with it. Helps with our energy consumption, they say. Well, when you wake up in the dark, you have to turn the lights on. That's using energy, isn't it? And it also seems like a waste of energy - mine - to go to all the trouble of changing all the clocks we have accumulated. I counted a total of 14 the other day. That's a lot of springing forward. Takes time to change time.

They tell us they're "saving" time at the beginning of the day so they can make more daylight at the end of the day. Doesn't make sense. What's the matter with daylight earlier in the day rather than later in the day.

And there's another factor. I would imagine some of the good people in White County and surrounding territories would probably agree that this time thing we're messing with is "God's time" and ought not to be messed with. Well, I guess He did cause this whole time thing to start ticking, but I doubt that the daylight savings creation matters much to Him. Probably matters most to the cows, what with milkers coming around an hour earlier by cow time, and fumbling around in the dark for a few squirts of milk.

Reminds me of a story I heard. A man asked God, "May I ask a question about time? How long is a million years to you?" God answered, "A million years is but a minute." "Well," continued the man, "how much is a million dollars to you?" Again God answered, "A million dollars is but a penny." The man asked, "Then would you grant me a penny?" God answered, "Let me think a minute." I doubt He spends half a minute thinking about DST.

However, I did some limited research on the matter and it produced the following: From ye ole encyclopedia - dated though it is - I found this ... "As a result of Daylight Savings Time, darkness comes one hour later than on standard time." Simply stated, don't you think?

But not to be outdone by simplicity, I went to the Internet and, to use tech-no-speak, I "googled" it, and found this declaration ... "It decreases the amount of daylight in the morning so more daylight is available in the evening." (I'm not making this up, folks.)

The idea began in Great Britain during the WW # I for economic reasons. Leave it to the British to start something. The U.S. made it legal over here in 1918, but Congress repealed it the next year, and had the good sense to leave it alone for almost three decades. After WW # II, Congress began to twist and turn in the night as well as day, and by 1966, DST became an annual nationwide adjustment, mostly. Except for Arizona and Hawaii, for some odd reason. The fine print didn't say why.

Now, they're starting it earlier and I'm back in the dark earlier, too. And it's darker in the mountains than on the flat land, I can tell you. One day, I fear, Congress will make it mandatory year-round. We'll all be in the dark earlier ..... along with Congress, which seems to stay in the dark, most of the time.

PART II -

CAN FAT GRAMS CAUSE THE "EPPAZOODICS?"

HEALTH CARE IN A STATE OF FLUX

It seems like I have been going to the doctor all my life and it always starts the same way. Something about me isn't working like it's supposed to, or I begin to hurt in some location in my body, or I just plain look and feel puny. So, I go to the doctor.

When I was a wee little boy, my doctor came to me. His name was Dr. Thomas and he was about 103 years old and carried a little black bag. He called me "punkin." He would come in my bedroom where I was about to die and put a thermometer in my mouth or one of those flat sticks on my tongue and ask me to say, "Aaaah." I don't remember what he ever saw or did, but I do know he finally quit coming. In fact, all my doctors quit coming.

Now, no doctor will come to see me, I have to go to them or die, whichever comes first. I think they quit coming during the days of Perry Mason. People in the law profession began to get ideas from that TV show and the doctors retreated to their offices for examinations and saying "aaah," where they felt safer..

Anyway, for decades now, I have been going to see the doctor and to be quite honest, it hasn't been such a bad experience. Most times, the man in white has taken care of what ailed me, I paid him or the bill came later, which wasn't too awfully much at first. Then one day, my boss man said he'd provide me some insurance through the Am I Blue Insurance Co. and I won't have to pay the doctor so much for his new yacht and stuff.

So then, I showed up at the doctor's office, and just gave the receptionist my card, waited an hour or two and saw the doctor for oh, say, for about five minutes or so and left. Didn't pay a nickle. Of course, the Am I Blue Insurance Co took a "pound of flesh" out of my paycheck, but I was happy and luckily, I'm still kicking.

Now, something new is showing up and it's coming out of Washington. You may ask, "Can anything good come out of Washington?" Well, I suppose it can. I read where a lot of people got a stimulus check. But I'm like Forrest Gump, when he was talking about his million dollar wound from being shot in the "but-tocks." He said, "I never did get any of that. The government must have kept that money." Today, it may be more fact than fiction.

From what I hear, they may be keeping our money to start this new public health care plan all the talking heads are talking about. But if they cover as many people as they say they will cover, they're gonna have to rob Peter to pay Paul's gall bladder bill, if, in fact, they even allow Paul to get his gall bladder examined. He may have stand in line with Marvin the plummer who needs a knee replacement.

Then it depends on which one wins the game of "scissors, rock, and paper" to see who goes to the front of the line for surgery. But before Nurse Ratchett makes you lie down on the gurney and whispers, "Little stick," you have to fill out forms about any pre-existing conditions, like, if you gambled away your allowance while playing pool, or ever smoked Camels behind the garage when you were a kid, any answer to which may cause you to have to "go directly to jail and don't pass Marvin" ever again.

And then, if you choose not to accept the money from Peter, he is free to keep it and use it to go to Canada where they have a nation-wide "Let's Make A Deal" health plan for everyone.

Who knows what else will be coming out of Washington? I guess we'll have to stay tuned.

WILL HEALTHCARE BILL COVER THE REAR FLANK?

In all probability, the new health care bill will not include coverage of some of the medical issues we see advertised on television. Like, what to do with the dreaded "E.D." strikes, or when your prostate gland swells to the size of a watermelon, or when you hear the downside of taking the newest pill which "may cause worms, distended navels, toe jam build-up, or lost of breathing for over three days. See your doctor if these occur."

Another problem, which may not be included, is the all-time worst exam of all. I was discussing this subject with a bunch of guys one morning recently over coffee. One of our group is in the throes of preparing for such an exam. He had recently met with his doctor who gave him the "preparation" for the procedure, which should be called a "Molotov cocktail."

I had such an experience some months back and wanted to be encouraging. At the beginning of one's concern, you think of, say, Milk of Magnesia. Then, maybe you go for something stronger. Then the "Prep H" factor comes to mind. Finally, you give in and make the dreaded appointment with your doctor. Except it isn't your regular doctor. It's a specialist with a mile-long title. It starts with "gas" and trails off towards the next county.

On the appointed day, the nurse brought me in the little room. I sat on the table with the crinkly white paper in a state of apoplexy for what seemed like an eternity, wondering when he'd show up … *behind* me. Finally, he came; he looked, and said, "Hmmmm, we probably need to take a further look." I knew exactly what "further" meant. I was a goner. I broke out in a cold sweat. Smiling, he gave me a sheet of information about my upcoming execution and left.

By far, the worst aspect of this procedure had to do with getting ready for it. The day before is agony. You can't eat anything – no peanut butter, no burgers 'n fries, no mashed potatoes and fried chicken. You can only have water, juice, and chicken broth, which tastes like unsalted hyssop. And, the kicker is you have to drink the required gallon of thick, pungent liquid which must have been imported from lower New Delhi. That's right, a *gallon*.

Getting that stuff down with no French fries for a chaser is indescribable. In addition to having no munchy tidbits throughout the day, there was no coffee the next morning before leaving for the "look-see" procedure. But like a good soldier, I showed up and was ushered into the examining room.

"Mr. Mason, please lie down on the gurney and turn on your side," the sweet nurse instructed. I felt a "stick" in my arm. I vaguely remember the doctor coming in. He spoke softly and carried a big hose - long enough to reach my esophagus, and disappeared behind me. Next thing I knew, he had come around in front and said, "All clear on the southern end." Well, actually, he didn't say just that, but he indicated I was okay.

In my discussion with the guys, one said that he had seen on television where someone who was enduring the same exam was able to listen to Lou Rawls singing, "You'll Never Know" in the background. I heard no melodious singing. No angels either, for which I was grateful. I lived through it to eat peanut butter again. Just not too much at one sitting.

But I still wanted to be encouraging to my friend whose endurance will be tested soon. I thought about saying, "Don't worry - it's a piece of cake." But knowing what he's in for, I didn't have the heart to use that metaphor.

CHEWING MORE AND ENJOYING IT LESS

There is one thing worse than the infamous colonoscopy exam where the doctor sneaks up on your blind side and goes searching through your innards with a very long hose. And that one thing is the extraction of a tooth.

A scene in the movie, "Castaway," depicts the main character, Tom Hanks, preparing for what he knows will be a painful ordeal. While marooned on a deserted island, which is bad enough, he develops a toothache. The pain becomes so intense, he decides to "extract" the tooth on his own. . . with an ice skate blade … and a large rock. Luckily, he succeeds, but there should have been a disclaimer saying, "Don't try this as home."

Once, while marooned in a dentist chair, I was told, "This tooth ought to come out. Your mouth may fall off one day." That was two years ago. I should have known better.

My mother who was a "stickler" for tooth maintenance and took me to Dr. Kirkpatrick regularly. He wore a white jacket and a smirk on his face and carried a big drill. Mother's teeth were good, and she wanted mine taken care of. Dad, on the other hand, had all his teeth pulled at once when he was young, poor guy. He was a "two-plate man." The thought of enduring that much pain always got me into Dr. Kirkpatrick's chair for cavity searches.

So, recently, the tooth in question became so bad that it seemed time to say goodbye to number 23. I thought of Tom Hanks, and my dad's teeth and decided to see my dentist like a good boy. As usual, he talked about what he might recommend - extract it, leave it a little longer, or have a tooth implant, a newer procedure where you to have to sell your house and most of your furniture to pay for it. A "bridge" was the most I could do and that meant no golf for a year.

Then he made his suggestion. "If it was my father, I'd say just take it out." *Father?* I wanted to yell. Young whipper-snapper! But I relented, and said, "Okay, let's do it."

He strapped me in the chair, leaned the chair back as the blood rushed to my head, sat down and used his famous dental line, "Let's numb it up." He then reached for the dreaded syringe which was as large as a jack-hammer and mumbled, "Little stick."

What is it about the medical profession? Do they have a class in med school called Little Stick 101? Take your blood, "little stick," get a flu shot, "little stick." Every doctor I go to these days says "little stick." This involved *two very big* sticks. Every muscle in my body tightened, I held my breath, sweat popped out in all the wrong places. Then he disappeared. I waited as #'s 21, 22, 25, and the whole right side of my mouth began to go to the land of nod.

Thirty minutes later - the longest half-hour in my life - he returned and began to do his excavation. Split it in two, chiseled the cap off, and took out one root at a time. Finally, it was over and my heart quit racing. He shook my hand and said, "See ya in six months for your bridge. Don't eat over there for awhile." I walked out with a baseball-size wad of gauze in my mouth.

I came back about six months later and he says, "You know, it might be a good idea to have a root canal on that tooth that supports the bridge. It's kinda 'iffy.'" He suggested another "specialist" to do the canal part. But now, I'm chewing more enjoying it less. The bridge may collapse any day.

The ghost of my mother still lingers.

FAT GRAM MANIA CAUSES CREATIVE MENU

Recently, I was eating my breakfast at a busy local restaurant and began thinking, as I do quite often these days, about fat grams. Specifically, how many fat grams were in this country ham biscuit I was chomping on? It has almost become an habitual culinary pattern for me to think about and check, if possible, the fat grams in my food.

You may be somewhat perplexed, if you've seen my thin frame, as to why I would be remotely interested in fat grams. Well, one of my doctors some years back suggested I become acutely aware of the little boogers after he cajoled me out of some of my blood and showed me my cholesterol number. It was close to Methuselah's age. He gave me a little book to keep tabs on the fat gram numbers of items like Wendy's Big Classic, Gummy Bears and matzoh balls.

So, when I got home, I checked the little fat gram book for biscuits. It listed numbers for *medium* size only. The "mountain" biscuit I ate does not come in medium, trust me. I checked those made with baking powder or buttermilk or Bisquick mix. Not sure which kind I was eating, but I think it was the big mix kind and was probably made with lard. Then I checked country ham. Not a good number. I should have known better. All you have to do is think about it's origin - *pig* - and you get an idea of the number of fat grams.

Well, in an effort to be fat gram cool, I thought it would be smart to order something to go along with my monstrous country ham biscuit that is a bit more healthy, such as oatmeal with raisins, to counteract the fat grams in the C H biscuit. I figure the good "fat," in this case oatmeal, counters the bad "fat," as in country ham biscuit, and I'd come out smelling more like a rose than a pig.

I have not shared this new creative eating custom with my current doctor who monitors my numbers periodically by having the lab check my blood with "a little stick" from Nurse Rachet who always carries a big needle. He would scoff and want to put me on some drug to combat my condition, which might cause something to happen in my liver or spleen or Gluteus Maximus or medulla oblongata. I am television-wise to those advertising tricks about "this medicine may cause … etc, etc". I have a straight line to the "Wizard of Oz, MD." She lives in my house and monitors the Oz man daily.

I will admit to even taking this eating pattern a step farther and, for example, ordering a supreme pizza one night, which probably has some 11,500 fat grams, and counteract the fat gram numbers with a meal the next night of fruits and salads, which have almost no fat grams. On occasion, I have even made it a one-night-counteraction meal, ordering, for example, two pork chops (see pig, above) with a bowl of rice (no fat grams) on the side. Cornbread might be optional unless it's made with lard, then you may be over the limit.

Still, the ever vigilant, fat gram police have succeeded in making me feel sufficiently guilt-ridden and so, I have become quite meticulous, as I peruse the grocery shelves, checking many of the items and their fat gram numbers. I am aware that too many people are carrying around a lot of fat grams, and I don't mean in their grocery carts.

But I can tell you it is not an easy proposition. When I am shopping and come to, say, the peanut butter section, I struggle as I count the many, many, fat grams on the jar. So,

I will counteract once again by reaching for the "low fat" graham crackers to spread the luscious peanut butter on. Peanut butter and low fat grahams … it's a good combination. Or should I say "counter-action."

NO FUN AT HOME WITH THE "EPPA-ZOODICS"

An old joke goes like this: A lion, king of the jungle, was strolling along when he came upon a lowly tiger. "GRROOWRR," roared the lion, "why aren't you as big as I am?"

The tiger lowered his gaze and said, "Uh, I don't know," slinking off in in the jungle in a trot. The lion then came upon a large rhino. Again the lion growls, "GRROOWRR, why aren't you as big as I am?" The rhino cowers and answers, "Gosh, I don't know," disappearing in the thicket.

Later that day, the lion comes upon a little mouse, slowly trudging down the path. The mouse's eyes are red, he's coughing, and holding a handkerchief over his nose. The lion blurts out once more, "GRROWRR, why aren't you as big as I am?"

The mouse squeaks, "I been sick."

Well, not to be too mousy, but I haven't felt big as anything lately, 'cause "I been sick." Don't mean to be complaining, but this ain't no fun. Everyone tells me, "Aw, it's really going around," or "Yeah, I had that last month and liked to never got over it," or "Man, my wife had that thing and coughed for two months. Stuff 'bout killed her."

Everybody's got a story of sick and there's kind of a one-upmanship that goes along with their stories. As I see it, however, there are different kinds of "sick." First of all, there's the "call-into-work-sick." I've had this type a couple of times. It was really difficult to make the call because of the overwhelming guilt I felt. It's a carry-over from eighth grade when you didn't have your book report ready for class and told your mama you were sick. I knew she'd catch me in a lie. I still wasn't too big to spank.

This kind of sick hits you on the spur of the moment two or three times a year. Sometimes it comes in the spring, when the dogwoods are blooming and it's the first day the temperature hits 70 degrees. It is amazing how four guys can get this at the same time and by 10:00 a.m. they are all feeling a lot better and basically over it by about the 5th hole.

Or it may come right around the 18th of December. Suddenly you feel deep chest pains and coughing just begins to come easily. You gotta call in sick because you realize there's only six days left before Christmas and the base of the tree is still rather bare reminding you that you haven't done one lick of Christmas shopping. You get the idea.

Another kind of sick is at the other extreme of the feel bad syndrome. It is what I call the "stay-in-your-jammies-in-the-bed-all-day-never-want-to-see-a-living-person-again" sick. This kind of condition usually lasts about two weeks and is generally caused from making the comment, "Aw, I never have had one of those flu shots and I'm not going to start now." You start looking over your will after about the 9th day. I had a sick like this in "the winter of '91" and swore on a stack of all the Bibles in my house that I would take a flu shot the rest of my years. "Jammie sick" is the pits.

The last example of sick I will mention is the one I have had recently. It is akin to what my father used to call the "eppa-zoodics." You don't feel you should be pajama bound all day. But you don't feel like raking leaves either. It is bad enough to make you think watching Paula Dean toss salad could be very interesting to you. You cough from down about as far as your ankles and wonder what else is living that far down that comes up the color of a buttercup.

POLITICAL CHIT-CHAT:
A CALL FROM THE SENATOR

The telephone rang the other afternoon and I immediately picked up, expectantly wondering who might be calling me. So often, it is for my wife and I just thought, maybe this time, it would be for me.

"Hello," I said, eagerly.

"Hello, this is Senator John McCain."

I actually couldn't believe my ears at first. I wanted to yell to my dear wife to pick up the other phone, that the Senator was on the line, but I was so awe-struck - sort of like the old Ray Stevens record called the "Streak" - as if I had been "mooned" and therefore caught almost speechless in the process.

He told me how happy he was to discuss his campaign with me. Actually, "discuss" is a misnomer - more like another short speech I remember by Old Ross Perot, who began, "Now, pay attention, this is simple," pointing with his stick to the flowchart on the wall.

The senator told me about his voting record during the past few years, and how he felt the war was going in Iraq, and what he wanted to do about that, reminding me of his own personal war experience, of course.

I tried to ask him a question or two, but he kept right on talking about his vision of health care and how he was going to handle our borders. I presumed he didn't mean the border between Alabama and Georgia, but with all the water wars going on, I wasn't sure. Maybe he had a plan for Lake Lanier.

He had such a soothing voice, lingering in my ear as he asked me to be on my toes as I cast my vote - hopefully for him - on Super Tuesday (my caps). I tried to get in another word and explain that I didn't need to stand on my toes for anything, because I was tall enough to reach the lever, or punch stick, or magic marker, whatever they have in the voting booth. But he heard not a word and I could tell he was about to wrap it up.

Anyway, before I knew it he said "Adios, Amigo" - not to be confused with any immigration farewell protocol - but merely a friendly good-bye. I hollered, "But wait!" into the phone, but it was dead, which was not at all how he sounded over the phone, as some have surmised. He sounded young and trust-worthy, as if he was having an intimate little chat with Mrs. McCain.

After hanging up, I mused to myself, poignantly, and began to think about other calls I have had from important contestants in political races and I came up with ... none!

Then I began to wonder, more logically, if I would ever get a call from, say, Mr. Romney. Probably not because I am not living in Massachusetts and I'm in a different tax bracket than he.

Again, I thought that because I have had extensive experience through the years working with Baptist preachers that I might get a call from The Reverend Governor Huckabee and he would give me his take on things political. But I've heard so many sermons in my day and I don't think I could handle "3 points and a poem" again.

Then there's Mr. Obama and his "change" thing. At my age I've had more things changing than I know how to deal with. No call from him. And then there's sweet Hillary... but I doubt that she would "feel my pain" enough to call me out here in White County and ask me about it. No call from her, either.

Where is Ross Perot when I need him? He could just keep it simple.

BASEBALL BOYS BEAT
OUT POLITICIANS

Let me give you some idea of how I feel about all the political announcements, advertisements, and recorded telephone calls of recent days. I have been watching a lot of baseball during the past three weeks or so. I'd much rather see a good 94 mph fast ball get a strikeout than hear someone lambast someone else who answers, "Yeah...you a 'nother one!"

As we all know, our poor Braves weren't in the big dance again, though they made a good run. World Series '10 had a couple of teams other than the Phillies, Yankees, Red Sox and Cardinals. Seems like one or two of those four are always in the Series. This time was different.

We had an unusually upscale team from Texas, who won the American League pennant. Nolan's boys. He of the "Ryan Express" fast ball of yesteryear, now president of the Rangers. To add to the Texas flavor, the fourth game featured the Great Bush Presidents ... numbers 41 and 43, father and son, which, as I said in the introduction of this book, hasn't happened in our country since the days of the Adams Family.

The foe from the National League was that once-ugly-team-from-New York, the Giants, who have languished away in the foreign land of San Francisco since 1958, and, I might add, have not won a World Series since. Which was all right with me, for I have hated the Giants since October, 1951. Let me explain.

When I was in high school, my team of teams was the Brooklyn Dodgers. In 1951, they had to play the Giants two out of three for the National league pennant. In the third game, Bobby Thompson hit a home run that won the game and the pennant for the Giants, who, of course, went on to lose the Series to the Yankees. The papers called Thompson's homer the "shot heard round the world," which, as you might know, was a line a sports writer stole from the poem by Ralph Waldo Emerson called "Concord Hymn."

Then, horror of horrors, both the Giants and the Dodgers packed up and were sent to the "Land of the Cal-EEE-fornians," as their governor so eloquently stated. So, as an adult, my whole baseball thing began to wane until I moved to Atlanta years ago and became a Braves's fan. All because of Bobby Thompson, may he rest in peace. (By the way, Bobby died in August of this year at his home close to Savannah, and didn't get to see his former team win their first series on the west coast.)

So, you can see my bit of angst at seeing the Giants win. I was kinda pulling for the Rangers because of our former Brave and ace good guy, Jeff Francoeur, who is now a Ranger.

But alas, the Giants celebrated and I have to put on a good face and utter such platitudes as, "the best team won," or "they had such good pitching," or "congratulations to the winner." Why?

Well, it's a family thing. Some of you know that my son lives in the Land of Cal-EEE-fornia, some 75 miles south of San Francisco. What that means is when we've talked recently, all he can talk about is the cotton-pickin' Giants, and Tim, and Edgar.

But then, as I said at the beginning, any baseball talk wins out over the political "yip-yap" that seems to be everywhere of late. Aren't you glad it's over. But as you know, it's only for a little while.

DEALS BY YOUR FRIENDLY GOVERNMENT DEALER

As you know, the automobile industry is experiencing some growing pains, along with an occasional funeral. Of course, this is not all that new. Remember the Studebaker, the Henry J, and that old stand-by, the Edsel, which stood by for only about two years, as I recall.

Over the years, we've had wake after wake for first one automobile or another but now it seems whole dealer/manufacturers are dying on the assembly vine. And with the cost of gas these days, what used to be that ole advertising staple to "See the U.S.A. in your Chevrolet," may one day get you only to Blairsville, Ga, by way of Hiawassee.

As a result of this, the High Potentate CEO of the newly created "Government Motors" - Sir Obama himself - has taken over and sent the message to "make that machine go clean and green." And what that means is get smaller, a bad sign for people like me who are "small car challenged." This does not bode well. One day, I may have to trade in my big Silverado pick-up for a Shetland Pony pick-ette.

Perhaps you read sometime back about three new such vehicles with very weird names which are coming down the pike. One is called the Cube. You remember the rubik's cube? It's about that small. It looked bigger than a breadbox in the picture, but not much. "See the U.S.A. in your Cube" doesn't seem to fit well. I could suggest..."Don't be a boob, buy a Cube." I doubt they would accept that.

Another model is called the Krom. Where do you think a Krom came from? I have no idea, but is sounds alien to me. Isn't that where Superman was born? If you were a teenager, would you go to "the prom in your Krom?" I don't think so.

The other vehicle they said was coming soon is called the Soul. I'm not sure how I feel about this car. This could be related to a spiritual matter that is nobody's business. I had a friend tell me one time about his car breaking down one night and he prayed and prayed that it would start, and lo, it did! I'm not doubting the Almighty's power at this point. But deep down in my soul, it would seem inappropriate for me to say, well, "Bless my Soul."

In addition to being small, they seem to be trying to sell us on the unique extras. For instance, there are "shag-carpet panel inserts, aerodynamic body kits, and front-door bungees" - for jumping, I guess. And, "illuminated kick plates, rear cargo organizers, and a fully integrated front and rear fascias, with body side sills, and a unique rear roof spoiler." I don't think I ought to get into all this, but they seem to be more interested in features toward the rear. I am interested in more leg room up front. My rear is fine, thank you.

The main concern for me is what to do with my rather lengthy legs and long feet in these new, smaller "green" cars. The very first Chevrolet I ever owned had lots of room and no hunky console. Just a small "vacuum shift" on the steering wheel. No "rear spoilers" to cramp your style. Now that the government is in the auto business, I'm afraid that one day, they could just come and confiscate my dear, roomy pick-up and say, "Hey, you ole rube, gotta drive a Cube."

As Kermit the frog would say, "it's not easy being green."

THIS "AVERAGE" JOE DEFINITELY NOT A PLUMBER

The media is taking liberties with my name again, this time dragging me through the current political mire. They're making sport of the "average Joe," in this case a poor plumber from Toledo, just trying to get by, getting caught outdoors asking Mr. Obama a simple question. Poor guy was just at the wrong place at the wrong time.

For some reason, they continue to lock on to my name. The "average Joe" this and the "average Joe" that. My earliest memory was of a comic strip called Joe Palooka. You know what a palooka is? An inexperienced, basically punch-drunk boxer, that's what.

Then when I was a little older I heard about the poor, average soldier back in "the waw-wuh," as Miss Scarlett called it, who was known as G. I. Joe, the more lowly ranked infantryman. He lay in the mud in the foxholes, poor guy. Looked about as bad as a soldier could look

There were other Joe's through the years that made me feel less than average, like, Joe the Six-pack, Joe Cool, and Joe Camel, who people began to view with disdain. Now, they're at it again with Joe the Plumber. Except for the fact that this is his real Joe. And he really is a plumber. I can imagine how he must feel, portrayed as an "average Joe" with the cameras bearing down on him. But they'll probably make a movie about him, so he'll come out okay.

Of course, I have never been a plumber. Never wanted to be. Don't know how that stuff works. Don't know an elbow pipe from a blown gasket. I've known other Joe the plumbers but I'm no plumber, as Lloyd Benson might have said to Dan Quayle today. So, truth be known, I'm glad there are a few Joe the Plumbers around. Takes some of the pressure off me.

What I want to know is why you don't hear, for example, about Dan the Plumber, or Horace the Plumber, or even Marvin the Plumber. It's always Joe. What's the matter with, say, Bruce. Now Bruce has a nice ring to it, seems to me. Bruce the plumber. Now, why didn't the good president-to-be, Mr. Obama mosey over and talk with Bruce the Plumber. Perhaps he lived across the street, or maybe down in Chillicothe. Call Bruce to fix your plumbing thing-a-ma-bob ... in this case thing-a-ma-Bruce.

Noooo, he has to talk to an average "Joe" who happens this time, not to be a palooka, or a six-pack, or a Camel, but a plumber. So, now I have become another average Joe again, poor guy and poor me.

Even one of the current vice-presidential candidates is yip-yapping about it. Here he is an "average Joe the Senator" just trying to get by with a vote here and a vote there, perhaps a bit upset because he had gotten upstaged on the camera by Joe from Toledo. That's the way those politicians do when they are upstaged.

He's probably thinking, "Here I am, ole Joe the Senator, finally get to the big time, standing here waiting, and after all this work on my transplanted hair roots, and he's talking to Joe the Plumber. What a bummer!"

Yeah, I know, Joe. It's tough being dragged through the media as another "average Joe." But as we all know, a little time goes by and the average Joe is forgotten. Joe the Plumber, have you heard of him lately? Probably messing with some commode somewhere in Ohio, poor guy.

And Joe the senator is just about to retire ... so he says. Ha!

SOMETHING ABOUT
TAKING CHANCE

There's not much humorous about this, but I'm going to tell you anyway.

Some weeks back, my wife and I spent a night on the road and while holed up in the motel, we saw a movie on HBO. It's usually our luck too see something putrid. The movie we saw this time was anything but.

It was entitled "Taking Chance" - a true story - and it was about a marine colonel who took on the responsibility for the first time of accompanying a fallen marine from the Iraq war to his hometown in Wyoming for burial. Most of us are not aware of what is involved in this duty and that became even clearer to the colonel, played admirably by veteran actor, Kevin Bacon. The marine's name was Chance Phelps.

I don't know what you think about war, Iraq, Korea, the military, et al. Personally, I've had my struggles with the whole matter, especially during my ministerial career. But I have always had a great respect for those who serve whether they joined or were drafted years ago.

It started when I was a child, growing up close to an army base in Western Kentucky. My parents rented a room to soldiers and their wives during WW II. So, I had an up-close-and-personal look at everything from their shiny belt buckle to how straight they walked to their fond goodbyes. Most of them I never saw again. But my memory of them is clear as a bell.

I suppose it was this background that caused me to sit up respectfully and watch the movie.

Some weeks later, a good friend invited several of us guys to his "basement theater," where he has a large screen and projector paraphernalia. He was showing this movie and I relished the chance to see it again.

This time, I sat in the company of "military men" of old … four former marines, and two army. I told them I had seen it and it was certainly worth another look. It was my personal observation that all of us sat in quiet awe of what we saw. It became a very moving experience to see the details of what happens to a fallen soldier in this country, and to watch the constant over-seeing respect the Bacon character portrayed during his duty.

It is not my intention to make more out of this movie than is there. In my opinion, it is worth your viewing. Because it was shown on HBO, you won't see it in the theater, but hopefully, it should show up at the video store soon.

Nonetheless, it was more significant to me seeing it a second time, if for no other reason than the audience of men I sat with. Perhaps, they were a gentle reminder of a long-ago childhood and my admiration for those who lived under the same roof as I. Or perhaps I was reminded of my fortunate or unfortunate "lot" of very limited service in the military years ago.

Suffice it to say, it was a privilege for me to watch this movie again and be able to sit among former marines and army men, all of whom I know I could count on if I needed someone to "take a chance with me."

I believe they are, like so many others, exactly what the slogan implies - Semper Fi ……"Always Faithful."

PART IV -

FAMILY STILL THE MOST IMPORTANT

ARE WE LOSING OUR DELICATE ETIQUETTE?

On Sunday morning, the pastor began his sermonic discourse on the subject of manners. I thought it was a bit elemental to begin with the subject of manners. But I sat and listened, mannerly. My pastor is a neat guy and I was sure he would come up with something unique.

In a humorous, yet mildly chastising way, he basically introduced the fact that manners in our society today are in serious want. I agreed and began to think of what I, myself, have noticed recently. Such as the young couple sitting down at the concert, as he walked in the row of chairs first, and plopped down with a slouch, while she come in after him carrying the bag of food, an extra lawn chair, with a kid in tow.

And on a recent trip, I was waiting for my food at a restaurant, when a family group came in and sat at a table close by. Almost immediately, the grandfather pulled out what appeared to be a Blackberry "smart" phone and started thumbing away. Soon, the younger son did the same with his. The grandmother ordered for everyone. The daughter sat silently and watched as the granddaughter piddled with her food. True, I didn't really know what was going on with them, but one could easily tell they did not know the meaning of manners, to say nothing about relating to each other.

Where is Emily Post when we need her. "Who?" you ask. Okay, she's dead and gone, leaving us way back in another era. The newest version, I suppose, is dear Martha Stewart. But she "got tainted" a few years back and spent some time in the "big house." That kind of tainting doesn't set well with the mannerly trend-setters. Guess we're on our own when it comes to this manners business.

When I was growing up, manners were a staple for us as we progressed toward adulthood. If you didn't adhere to some regimen of mannerly behavior, you were thought to be un-couth and could possibly be guilty of one of the seven deadly sins - being *sloven*. Oooo, sin and corruption.

My blessed mother, may God rest her gentle soul, was from the central hills of Kentucky and I came up with a philosophy, yea, even theology, that said "Stand up straight, hold your shoulders back, have a firm handshake, and tuck your shirt tail in, Joe Sidney."

But the real "etiquette generals" of my life were two aunts who lived in another small town not too far away. When I visited them, I was always at attention. Spinsters all their lives, they were known for their proper way of doing things. When an adult business associate spoke to me, I had my instructions, to wit, stick out my little hand and say, "Hidy-do, Mr. Murray." Lots of Yes sirs, and Yes ma'ams, and always, "tuck your shirt tail in, Joe Sidney."

You sat up straight at the table, you could only talk when someone else wasn't, and you always say "Please" when passing something. No whistling, no television watching when eating, and blackberries were okay, but you had to wait til you finished your dinner to have some in a bowl with sugar or in a cobbler.

Admittedly, I have not stayed up on my P's and Q's as I should and sometimes I don't tuck my shirttail in as I should, but I never, never wipe my nose on my shirt sleeve. Martha may not care, but the preacher could be watching. I might end up being an illustration in his next sermon.

MOTHERS KNOW HOW TO "GET IN YOUR HEAD"

Not that I am a sexist person, but I've got to say that women probably won't understand this. So, let me hasten to say that men and their mamas have some kind of special bond that will forever transcend any other relationship.

Let me give you some examples. Take Michael Oher. Do you know who he is? If not, see the movie The Blind Side. Oher was "picked off" the street by Leigh Anne Tuohy, played by Sandra Bullock, and "motherly" groomed him to grow up and ultimately become an NFL football player with the Baltimore Ravens. If there was ever a mother figure who made a lasting impression, it was Tuohy.

And then there's Gloria James. Mother of LeBron. If you have heard of LeBron, you might know that this year, he received his second straight MVP award for an NBA basketball player and the first person he praised was his mom, who raised him after birthing him when she was 16 years of age.

And regardless of what you think of Presidents Bill Clinton, George W. Bush, or Barrack Obama, you know enough about each one to know that they were significantly influenced for good by their mamas.

My favorite comic strip in the newspaper is called Zits. It's about a 16-year-old teenager named Jeromy and the battles and issues he has with his mom. Recently, Jeromy was listening to his weird friend with the pink hair and ring in his nose who is always "up to something." His friend looked in Jeromy's ear and said, "Wait," and proceeded to literally pull his mom out of Jeromy's ear. He sent her on her way and said to Jeromy, "You're no fun to talk to until you get your mom out of your head."

That's one of the things moms are good at ... getting in your head. It's that mothering instinct that pervades the space in your head you know you should have filled up with just exactly what she told you before she told you. It's as if she takes up lodging in that space and is, well, "in your head." Most times she doesn't leave and thankfully, you remember from time to time what she instructed you to hear.

Whatever she imparts through the years can be very valuable along life's highway. She gives you instructions on how to take a good bath. She pelts you with a clean under-wear persona. She makes you think it's important to take piano lessons. She blesses you with the art of worrying. She humbles you with lessons on crying. No one can cry quite like a mother and when you cause your mama to cry, you never forget what a dastardly deed you have committed.

She gives you little tidbits, like, "don't smack your mouth when you chew" - "hold your shoulders up" - "don't forget your handkerchief" - "pick up your socks" - and "use your napkin." No one else in the world can get away with those commands but your mama. Not even a platoon sergeant.

Like I say, they get in your head and, if we're lucky, they become implanted. True, you may leave them, or on some occasion, they may leave you. But that special remnant of your mother will never leave. She's in your head - for good.

Some years back, I went to visit my mom in her "holding cell," just this side of heaven. While sitting in her wheelchair in a daze, she suddenly turned to me and asked, "Joe, are you happy?"

There was only one answer - yep, you're in my head, Mom.

FATHERS ARE ALWAYS
IN DEEP TAPIOCA

So, Father's Day comes around the corner every year. I can hardly wait. Let's see, where will I have my big Father's Day dinner, at my daughter's home or my son's home. Or will they, per chance, come to my house bearing shirts and ties and endless golf balls, along with covered dishes of sumptuous recipes to delight my "tummy-heart?" Someone pinch me, I must be dreaming.

As you know, this is the day of the year which probably should have been named, the "Other Parent's Day." I mean, what's left after Mother's Day? That's the biggy, right? Roses, corsages, wining and dining at elegant eateries, even the wayward son who lives in the commune in Idaho flies in to see Mama. The loving daughter bakes a big cake, *all by herself.*

Then, five weeks or so later, when it's hot, and everyone wants to go to the lake, or fishing, or to the beach, we have Father's Day. Don't forget to get a loving card and the box of golf balls. That'll do it. Let's meet at the Waffle House after church. Maybe they won't be able to make it to church but "I'll just meet ya at lunch."

It's not that we fathers aren't important in the scheme of family things. Problem is, there's just a lot of "residue" from the days of growing up with father that hangs in the air. Subtle memories of making you find a job when you wanted to merely hang out with friends. Or, his reaction when you came in and your nose was pierced with a ten-penny nail. Or, his disdain when you wore flip-flops to church. So, I tend to think that fathers stay just a hairs-breath away from being mired up in a "deep bowl of tapioca."

And there's always the "father-always-liked-you-best" syndrome. Sometimes the giant baby cookie-cutter cut a tough deal. You had three girls and then a boy. You think the girls have a chance? The boy is always king. Or, if it was the other way around - two or three boys and one girl. "Daddy's little girl" gets everything, right? No one takes the place of the princess.

If you are a lonely only, as I was, there's a little some-thing hanging in the atmosphere that wonders what it would be like if there was a daughter around. You get a clue when you come home wearing an earring, and your dad likes it. Or if you're the girl and only child, Dad comes home and says, "Wanna go huntin' this week-end, sweetie." Subtle clues that give off the message that he sure would like to have a son, right?

And of course, fathers deal with their image, also. We always think we're in charge or try desperately to be, but deep down we know we aren't. "You wanna go to California!! There's nothing but flakes and nuts and a terminator for gov-ernor!! A rock band??? Are you crazy?" Or, "Your boyfriend wants to be an artist? Mercy sakes! What's the matter with Hedley, that nice chap with a degree from Tech, whose parents live in Buckhead." Fathers have a tough time with being dif-ferent. We all want stability and a good image.

Talk, cajole, and plead all you want. You're stuck in a deep bowl of tapioca. It all comes back to haunt you on Father's Day. We can't escape the inevitable. Sloggin' around in the bowl.

I have one of each, a boy and a girl. They're man and woman now, but to me, they'll always be a boy and a girl.

Someday, one may say to the other, "Ya know, I think Daddy always liked you best," and they'll have a few laughs. One thing's for sure. They know that I love them both more than life itself.

THAT FIRECRACKER WILL PUT YOUR EYE OUT

In addition to being patriotic this week-end, there'll be an obligatory fireworks show or two. How long has it been since you shot off a firecracker yourself? Gotta be careful handling those suckers.

Poor Ralphie always got an earful about B-B guns in the cute movie, "The Christmas Story." Many a boy has gotten the same earful about firecrackers, too. I speak from experience. My mama gave me a lot of instructions about fireworks. Mainly, she said not to play around with them, or I'd lose a finger, hand or worse. Sparklers was about as far as she'd go and always, "turn your head and close your eyes," which meant you didn't get to see the sparkles, rendering the thing pretty useless.

I didn't want to lose a finger or any other body part, for that matter, but Daddy always had a Roman candle or two come New Year's Day or July the 4th. He'd stand on the stoop and shoot that thing off, while Mama hollered inside, "Roy, you'll blow your finger off!"

Our neighborhood bully, Carl, who looked old enough to be drafted in those days, would throw them at us when he got the chance. He had a weird looking thumb, the nail of which curled back underneath, pointing toward his palm. He probably got it blown off with a firecracker, but nobody ever had the nerve to ask. Just the mention of his name struck fear in our hearts.

Most of us could get our hands on a few firecrackers for the July 4th holiday and occasionally, someone would come up with cherry bombs. They'd send a tin can thirty feet in the air and blow a tomato to smithereens.

Then one day, the American Civil Liberties Union was created and began pin-pointing the fireworks people and the politicians began making laws about how old you had to be and who and where and what time you could shoot off fireworks and some states banned them, probably because they were made in China and it seemed like about the only place you could buy them was at various spots along the Tennessee state line.

But low and behold, the other day, I saw this big tent over in the parking lot of the "other Wal Mart" not too far away, advertising "Fireworks for sale here." I stopped by to check it out, and found out that there were no firecrackers or cherry bombs. They did have some sparklers and a chubby, shorter version of the Roman candles that I remembered. Mostly, they had exotic box-sized "shower sparklers" and other such paraphernalia.

"Got any firecrackers?" I asked. "Nope." I asked another person if she knew if there were state laws governing their use and she seemed to have no idea what I was talking about, but that I could probably get some in South Carolina. "They don't have any regulations over there. You can get whatever you want there." I didn't want firecrackers that bad.

I talked with an official in Cleveland about county regulations and he told me whatever they are in the state is what we observe in the county. Said something about making loud noises and being a nuisance to neighbors if you wake them up late at night, disturbing the peace and all that.

So, go over to Helen or Demorest and take your lawn chairs and see someone else's big fireworks show. Enjoy the 4th that way and save your fingers.

THIS CARD GAME AIN'T YO DADDY'S POKER

Some time ago, an issue came up when it was "strongly suggested" that I take bridge lessons. I have never taken lessons for any other card game. Just explain a few details and I would soon pick it up. Not so with bridge. I found out during the lessons that bridge is not yo daddy's five-card stud poker.

I realize that the mere mention of the word, bridge, will send most men to the sports section or the letters-to-the-editor page. In fact, I would hasten to say that most men view bridge as a woman's game. It is true that women know bridge like "Bo used to know football." They are wired for the game of bridge - make that "hot-wired" - meaning they can talk the trumps and walk the trumps.

Most men, on the other hand, are out of their league at a bridge table. They don't know how to talk trumps, bid trumps, or count trumps. They struggle just coming to terms with all the talk, which women love to do while playing. Let's just take "the dummy," for instance.

Though men may at certain times be the very personification of this term, most who play this game sometimes struggle with being called "the dummy." Women, however, love for the man to be the dummy. They gain a certain edge in out-bidding their male partner, thus dubbing him "the dummy" for that particular hand, though I cannot document this. Just a hunch.

Some men, however, excel at the game of bridge. These men tend to be very smart, educated in an Ivy league school, quietly cocky, but sly as a fox. Some may even harbor a secret love for beating the woman at her own game, though I cannot document this. Just another hunch.

Up to now, I have not actually played much bridge. I am still a beginner, a lowly neophyte at this game, hence the lessons. I have been playing some with a few select people of similar skills, i.e., shuffling cards, separating spades from clubs, and learning to "pass" when it comes around for me to bid. My dear wife, the consummate bridge aficionado, has been most encouraging (see "strongly suggested" above) and accompanied me to the class. .

The class was composed of a rather large contingent of women and four men, one of whom remembered, after the first session, a standing golf game he had the same day of the week as the rest of our classes were meeting, hence he vacated the premises. The other two men were cool and quiet, like I said, sly as a fox.

However, I felt a close connection to one man when the teacher explained how to follow a "bid of two no-trumps, after you had bid with one club early on, followed by your opponent having passed." It was so complicated, he said he felt like "his whole life was passing before his eyes."

What I discovered was, in order to play bridge well, you have to read your partner's mind. When she bids two spades, you had better know exactly what she has in her hand so you can bid into a perfect fit with her cards.

This is similar to a discussion at the supper table when she asks a leading question and you respond with "Huh?" Then she utters that famous line, "You know what I'm talking about!" Bridge is very similar. When bidding, you had better know what she knows you ought to know, if you know what's good for you. You can be banished to yo daddy's poker for life.

My advice about the game is to just be "the dummy." You don't actually play the cards and you also have time to leave and use the facilities.

IN THE OLD DAYS OF "SIR" AND "MA'AM"

Most parents of any worth have a way of getting their message across to their children. "In the old days," a phrase I now use with great credibility, there was the switch, razor strap, belt, paddle (with holes for effect), or the lines "I'll take you to the woodshed" or "wait 'til your dad gets home" - any one of which could get the parent's message across.

Nowadays - a perplexing era for those who still deal with "the old days" - parents use virtually no item, not even the hand, and resort to phrases or "commands" (ha) such as, "I'll have to place you in time out," or "no television between 4:30 and 5:15 this afternoon," or "let me get back to you on that after we have our family conference," all of which *may* assist in getting the message across. Watching Dr. Phil and adhering to his pontifications could also be a good prerequisite for other means of communicating messages to children.

Anyway, one bit of mannerly advice I ingested as a child was the instruction to say "Sir" and "Ma'am." to my elders, all of whom were of the adult variety. This included aunts, uncles, teachers, neighbors, Sunday School teachers, coaches, the barber and even the postman. There were no post women "in the old days."

I caught on to this teaching very quickly, having a strong aversion to pain. I could "yes sir" and "no ma'am" almost professionally. It became my mantle of boyhood maturity, i.e., cute little boy wearing short pants, sticking his hand out with a "How do you do, sir." My parents were proud. My dad's parental motto was "I speak softly and carry a big stick" which was on the shelf in the garage and always within reach.

So, when I became a parent myself I figured I needed to pass this sage advice on to my two children. For some reason, it never took with either of them. Of course, I could not bring myself to use a belt or paddle, and I had no idea what "time out" meant, except on the basketball court. I finally gave up and, thankfully, they made it to adulthood fine without a passel of "yessirs" and "yes ma'ams." Just a "yeah" here and an "uh-uh"there along with an occasionally curt "yes" or "no."

Back to "nowadays," the perplexing era. It seems everyone I meet today is addressing me as "sir." May I help you, sir - here's your change, sir - just a stick with the needle, sir - et al, infinitum. I took a young minister at my church who is in his mid 30s to lunch recently. I never heard so many "sirs" in one sitting. I wanted to tell him to forget the sirs, but I didn't want to mess with his "timeout" up-bringing.

The other day, I was eating a biscuit at a local eatery here in Cleveland and traipsed over to get some more coffee. An elderly man (I figure anyone who *looks* older than I think I look, must be elderly) walked out of the rest room, slipped around, passed me and said, "Hello, sir." There I stood, wearing a ball cap, floppy T-shirt, shorts, and tennis shoes. Do I look like a "*sir?*" "Hiya doin'" would be fine. "Whzzz happening?" is okay. Or "Hey, man." But too many "sirs" reminds me of "the old days." Maybe, in my present day state, I seem to remind everyone of the "old days?"

I'm just used to another era of greetings. If I had walked in the house after school "in the old days," and addressed my dad with "Hey, man, what's happening?" I would have had some serious "time out" time in the woodshed, and maybe followed by a brief stay in ER.

PART V -

THE BENEDICTION

DOES YOUR SCROOGE MENTALITY NEED AN ANGEL?

Have you been "Scrooged" yet? You know, the Christmas season would not be complete without seeing the story of Ebenezer Scrooge somewhere, either at the movie, or on stage, or on one of the television channels that show the annual Christmas movies each year.

As you know, the story comes from the novel by Charles Dickens, A Christmas Carol, which he wrote back in the middle of the 19th century, around the1840s. He published the story himself and probably had no idea how popular it would become over the years to come.

We saw two movie versions in one night recently. The first was "A Christmas Carol," an old version, maybe the first ever filmed in 1938 starring Reginald Owen. Then we watched the musical version, entitled, simply, "Scrooge," which came out in 1970 and starred Albert Finney. We hope to see the 1984 version of the same story with George C. Scott one of these nights.

Everyone has a favorite. My favorite Ebenezer character is played by Finney, though I'm not too crazy about his singing. I also think Marley's ghost played by Alec Guinness in the same movie is the best portrayal of Scrooge's late partner. It's difficult for me to get wrapped around the George C. Scott character of Scrooge because I can't get his "Patton" role out of my mind. I keep thinking someone will salute him.

Suffice it to say, they all portray ole Ebenezer and his miserly, cranky spirit quite appropriately and if we'll admit it, one which we pick up from time to time. So, the question

I would pose today is how significantly do you or I really identify with the Ebenezer character? Well, most of us don't identify with his "stash of cash." But what about his attitude?

Do we ever have a tendency to "humbug" anything? Do we ever say to ourselves - because we'd be too embarrassed to say it out loud - "they ought to go ahead and die and decrease the population," one of the abundant Scrooge comments of the story. Scrooge gave a "bah, humbug" to little ole ladies, charities of most any kind, little children, poor Bob Cratchit, his faithful helper, and even his former partner, Jacob Marley, who had died a few years before after being worn down by his boss. Old Scrooge had a problem with just about everybody, even his closest and only kin, the nephew.

When it comes to the cold, hard business world, one could make a case for saying that Ebenezer was successful at being a frugal entrepreneur. But as it turned out, he lost out on so many other blessings of life, and finally came down to having just about no friends … nada.

Had it not been for the three "angels" who got his attention on Christmas Eve, he would have lived and died as just another "old poop."

Then, there's the other movie we get all taken by during the Christmas season … "It's A Wonderful Life." Little bit of a different twist, but when poor George Bailey develops his lousy "Scrooge" attitude, he ends up being saved by another angel, one Clarence Odd-body, who finally gets George's attention and turns him into a new person, using a phrase at the end, "No man is a failure who has friends."

Like Scrooge, he got saved by an angel at the last minute. Makes you wonder why we talk so much about angels during the Christmas season. So, pay attention. You may need an angel one of these days.

HANDLING THE FALL-OUT
OF FALSE WITNESS

When I was a kid playing "cowboys and Indians," Carl, the neighborhood bully, was always Gene Autry and I, along with the other neighborhood lesser-lights was an Indian. And when we had a gun battle, Carl got to shoot everybody and when Carl shot you, you had to fall on the ground "dead." Let me say, you'd *better* fall on the ground

One time, he shot at me and I didn't fall. "I got ya! "Carl shouted. "You're dead!" Which meant I should fall. I kept running on my stick horse and hollered back, "You missed me!" He hollered again, trailing close behind. "No I didn't," he claimed, gaining on me, *"you're dead!"*

"You lie," I yelled on a dead run around the corner of the house. Well, I think I really called him a liar. That wasn't the most appropriate thing to say to Carl, the neighborhood bully. When I came around the house again, I remember falling like a good Indian was supposed to, and "Gene Autry" was not straddling his horse, Champion, but rather, me, the name-calling Indian.

That experience taught me rather vividly that it's not in one's best interest to holler out that someone lied, whether they did or not. As you probably know, another guy named Joe tried to get away with using the same tactic recently while listening to Sir Obama give his speech to Congress. It would have to be another Joe dragged through the mire. But that's another matter.

The Good Book has a lot to say about bearing false witness, and as you know, it is one of the ten commandments which some people want to stick up on the court house wall, or plaster on a billboard, or maybe on their bumper. I'm not too keen on having the commandments on my bumper, because I'm just liable to hit a pothole and break one of those rules in public. Then someone would see me and shake a finger at me for not following my own bumper rules.

For example, I remember a few times in my "checkered" past when a policeman here and a policeman there pulled me over on the road for exceeding the speed limit. One time I didn't believe the information the policeman so authoritatively shared with me which caused him to come after me and pull me over. I wanted to say in my rebuttal, "You lie." But realizing my sitting position behind the wheel plus the badge he was sporting, to say nothing of the large-size pistol he was wearing on his hip, I acquiesced and kept my mouth shut. Thankfully, I didn't have to apologize before a jury of my peers which as you know, was the fate of the other Joe.

This is not to postulate in any political direction - one way or another - but I would imagine most presidents through the years have created a little "white lie" when they thought it necessary, or at least developed some questionable equivocation to make their points. Why, I myself have attempted on an occasion or two to be more eloquently creative while elaborating on my most recent, magnanimous golf shot, for example.

However, responding to one's prevarication of note out in public, in front of God and everybody, with a loud outburst, as if calling his bluff, ranks pretty close to that ole Forrest Gump phrase that was uttered in the movie a decade or so back, to wit, "stupid is as stupid does."

And it reminds me, vividly, of what my old coach said more than once to us kids on the basketball team years ago … "Boys," he would say, cinching up his khaki's, "the less you say, the less you have to take back." Selah.

WHAT PREMIUM DO YOU PLACE ON LAUGHTER?

Don't know about you, but things seem to be a little bit too serious. Oh, I know, we're living in serious times, and that causes people to be more solemn. Kinda like the dude that was wandering along, and a passerby said, cheerily, "Isn't it a beautiful day!" To which the dude retorted, "Yeah, but it's raining somewhere." Too many are responding that way today.

Need to turn that around, friends. Like, walking along in the pouring rain and a passerby says, "Isn't it an awful day!" And then we could say, "Yeah, but the sun is shining somewhere!" When things look bad, we have a tendency to look bad, too. Need to turn it around.

Let me give you a few ideas to consider. There's a proverb in the Bible that says, "A happy heart makes a cheerful countenance." Which seems to mean, if you feel good inside, you're going to show it outside. The late musician, Victor Borge, once said, "A smile is the shortest distance between two people." What brings folks together in a more congenial way? Nothing like a smiling, laughing person to make you feel better.

Many years back, when I was still stumbling about, I came upon an artistic sketch in an arts and craft store up in Gatlinburg which said, "Laughter is God's hand on the shoulder of a troubled world." Don't know who drew it or came up with the quote originally, but I bought it and framed it and it remained as if embossed upon my mind from then til now.

Whatever your faith-journey conjures up in your mind, heart, and soul about God - His creative genius, His all powerful, all present nature, His heavenly Being - it would be difficult *not* to believe that the Creator has "gifted" us with a unique ability to laugh ... . at ourselves, at the humorous situations in life around us, and at the sometimes "blunder-ful" manner in which we see new and humorous discoveries in our world. What a pleasant, divine diversion laughter can be in this "serious" world we live in today.

There's another factor about laughter which many folks may not have picked up on. And that has to do with the aspect of the "feel-good" nature of laughter. The late writer of yes-teryear, James Thurber, once said that "humor provides emotional chaos, remembered in tranquility." When you think about what happens in your body when laughter bursts forth, you have to consider those straining muscles, bursts of air from your lungs, jaws stretching from ear to ear, and stomach tightening, all from knee-slapping, "chaotic" laugh-ter. And when it's over - even momentarily - you have this boy-I-needed-that feeling. Like a dose of happy medicine.

Yes, life is serious, but look for the funny side. It's all a matter of getting things in a proper perspective. Like the col-lege coed, about to finish her junior year. Her parents were looking forward to having her home for the summer, but instead, they received this letter ... "Dear Mom and Dad, I won't be coming home this summer and, though this is not the best way to tell you, I needed to say that Johnny and I felt we should marry. In fact, we got married last week-end. And the main reason is because I am pregnant. You may not understand, but don't worry. We'll be living with his parents in the basement apartment and will come see you when the baby comes. Don't worry, we'll be fine. Much love, Amy

P.S. Mom and Dad, what you just read is not true. I got a D in Chemistry and I wanted you all to get things in their proper perspective."

So, when your big party is just getting started and it's pouring down rain, remember, "Smile, because the sun is shining somewhere."

SEARCHING FOR THE NEW
AMONG THE OLD

A-ha! Another new year. And what are you going to be about for this Year of our Lord, number 2009?

It is a profound and noteworthy question I should ask myself as I round the bend and begin again. Merciful heavens, can I even do that ... . "begin again?" 'Tis only the calendar that calls us to the "new," for, most of that which was with us in the "old" is still with us for the "new."

For example, we'll soon have a new president and his newly appointed politicos, all standing in a row on the platform. But in all probability, they'll perform with much of the old mannerisms and nuances that we have been used to, with the same general rhetoric that we've been used to, resulting in the same general grumbling from those who liked the "old" and question the "new."

Perhaps it's just a symptom. We search for something new but somehow it is still identified with the old. Many people will be searching for gainful employment, only to become employed down the road and still find themselves in the same kind of rut they were in before.

Some, like myself, will search for a better way to lower their golf score - a different ball, a newer club, some tips from an instructor - only to find the same old slice or hook or putting method that is still ingrained within us. The old makes life difficult for the new.

Also, we have all searched by making an annual litany of proposed new year's resolutions to make our lives better by eating a little less or a lot less, quitting smoking for good, going to church more regularly, spending more time with our children, learning a new hobby, reading more and watching television less, or changing an attitude that needs changing.

Sometimes, we find the needed adjustment, but not enough adjustment to really make any difference. The "old" raises its ugly head and overwhelms us so that we succumb even more to its ways. Oh, the dread in the phrase, "time marches on." It begs for the new, but keeps running into the old.

Would that we could turn back the clock. We are constantly searching for ways to keep time from marching so fast. We want it to go backward but it keeps moving forward. Sometime back, a new movie came out about a person named Benjamin Button. He ages in a backward fashion. Fictional, thank goodness, but intriguing nonetheless. Ole Ben starts out old and ends up new.

Imagine being a teenager with used up hormones. Or a senior adult being told by his mother to "turn off that music and finish your homework!" The search for the right age is an elusive premise.

George Carlin, the late bawdy comedian, wrote once that our expressing of aging changes as the years go by. When you're young, you want to be old he had said. "I'm 6, going on 7"- "I'm 13 and a half" - "I'm soon to be 21." But then we "turn 30, push 40, reach 50, make it to 60, and *hit* 70." The search for the new keeps bumping up against the old.

So, happy the New Year, whatever year it may be. But remember, Ecclesiastes says, "there is nothing new under the sun." Keep searching. It's a wonderful journey.